Sippies, Bubbles, & Big Fun

Oodles of Options for Rochester Families

Written by Kyra Bell and Vicki Tiede
Illustrated by Kate Badger

T.D.B.B. Publishing Inc.
Rochester, MN

Sippies, Bubbles and Big Fun

All Scripture verses are taken from the New International Version of the Bible.

Editors: Kristen Gabel and Laura Ehling

Cover Design and Interior Illustrations: Kate Badger

In loving memory of
Claire Elizabeth Brinker
September 21, 2002 – September 26, 2002

Jesus said, "Let the little children come to me, and do not hinder
them, for the kingdom of heaven belongs to such as these."
~Matthew 19:14

Meet the Moms

Kyra ~ A tour of my family: Mike (gracious husband), Kyra (wife/mom-in-training), Drew (4 years old) and believes we work for him, Claire (bountiful blessing in heaven) and Callan (4 months) and freely gives big smiles and giggles. Currently, I work very part-time as a dental hygienist for a local, dental group practice; I can't thank the staff enough for all of the support I receive from them to be a stay-at-home mom 90% of the time. My church family at Berean Community Church has become our "family" since our families don't live near us. The terrific moms I have met through MOPS over the last four years have been a blessing. My "transplanted friends"-you know who you are. Also, last but not least, to our "adopted family", the Tiede's. Especially to my Vicki, sister in Christ and sister of my heart; big smooches to you GIRLFRIEND!!!

Vicki ~ Mike is my love, rock, encourager, and superman, Kadi (9 years old) is my delightfully precocious pre-teen, Ben (4 years and Drew's best buddy) is my deep thinker, and Caleb (2 years) is my silly snuggle-bug. I am excited to be a busy, full time stay-at home mom. I home school my kids, tutor several other children and am a Council Coordinator for MOPS International for Southern Minnesota. My speaking ministry, Grace Lessons (www.gracelessons.com), provides me opportunities to encourage and equip women to face life's inevitable challenges: marriage, motherhood, and walking with Christ. Our family is blessed to call Berean Community Church home and the people there our friends. I am so thankful for the love and support of my parents. We are especially thankful for the Brinkers who actually understand the Tiedes! To my Kyra...you are right (again) ... we will be friends forever because you know too much! I thoroughly enjoy sharing dreams and detours with you on this journey we are on. Whatever's next, you bring the chocolate, I'll bring the java!

Meet the Illustrator

Kate ~ Lucky is the person who can make business out of play, and play is what my business, "Doodles by Doty", is all about. As a Minnesota farm girl, I learned early that when you live in the country sometimes creativity is your best friend. I spent much of my childhood scribbling light-hearted animals and children on scraps of paper and in notebook margins. These doodles followed me to Iowa State University where I studied art and design, eventually graduating with a degree in education. After eight years as an elementary teacher, I am now a freelance artist working in several different mediums including; painting, illustration, muraling, and graphic design.

My home is in Des Moines, Iowa where I live with my loving and supportive husband, Jamie, my two sweet little boys, Jacob and Benjamin, and our scruffy dog, Teddy. Life is good!

Preface

You may be wondering who these two "crazy" moms are and what made them set out on such a task? Well, I will share a little secret with you; we are crazy! Crazy about our kids and families! Drew and I have had the best time experiencing all the different things Rochester offers and have felt blessed by them. What motivated me to put this down in writing was a conversation with a mom who was on maternity leave with her second child. During story time at Barnes & Noble, she shared that she would be returning to work part-time. With extra time on her hands, she wondered what Rochester offered during the week for her to experience with her kids. I knew how she felt. There was actually a time in my life when I had never set foot in a McDonald's Playland! (Can you imagine that?)

Staying at home, either on maternity leave or as a stay-at-home mom can be lonely when there is little adult contact for mom. While sitting in the sandbox at the local park I have met some really interesting moms. It is so rewarding to have an instant bond with those moms because of our shared understanding of this season of life. Enjoy! ~Kyra

When Kyra suggested that we write a book and compile our favorite mothering trade-secrets, I told her that she was, in no uncertain terms, "CRAZY!" She just laughed and said, "So, which chapters are you going to write?" Within a few months of delivering my third child, we were writing this book. It has been so much fun and we hope that you enjoy this treasury as much as we enjoyed pulling it together. "Sippies, Bubbles, and Big Fun: Oodles of Options for Rochester Families" is so named because we have spent so much time filling and finding sippy cups, blowing bubbles, and having fun with our children here in Rochester, MN.

Now, enjoy your children. Enjoy this book. Enjoy sippies, bubbles, and big fun, while you raise your little ones and enjoy oodles of options for Rochester families. ~Vicki

Acknowledgements

We'd like to express a heartfelt thanks to all of our friends and family members for their support and encouragement during this adventure. A special thanks to our editors, Laura and Kristen. We appreciate the time and energy they invested in this project. Most importantly we give praise and thanks to our Savior who comforts, strengthens, and encourages big dreams which glorify Him.

Special Notes

This book is based upon our personal experiences and research. Some of the chapters are very specific to Rochester and all that it has to offer. Other chapters are more geared toward juggling life when you have little ones at home. While we have made every effort to provide up-to-date and accurate information, the world changes constantly and we can assume no responsibility for oversights, inaccuracies, or discrepancies. You are the best person to determine the needs, interests, and desires of your family, and we encourage you to employ your good judgment before you use any of the ideas or suggestions in this book.

We hope that this book is just the beginning of big fun for your family. By no means were we able to exhaust the possibilities that Rochester has to offer and we hope that you will add your own ideas, recipes, activities, and favorite places in the margins and on the blank pages of this book. Our prayer is that your copy of "Sippies" will be dog-eared, coffee-stained, and well-loved, for many years, by you and your family.

Finally, it is our desire for this book to be a blessing and benefit to all families in Rochester. We recognize that primary care-givers are not always moms, but include dads, grand-parents, and guardians. We celebrate this diversity, but to avoid confusion for the reader (and to be frank, for the authors) we occasionally refer to our readers as females.

Table of Contents

Enjoying Family Time

at Home

"This is the day the Lord has made;

Let us rejoice and be glad in it."

Psalm 118:24

Two of the most precious gifts you can give to your children are

your time and attention. Psalm 127:3 says "Children are a gift

from the Lord; they are a reward from him." It is our privilege to

spend time with our kids. As a mother, your time is valuable, so

spending time with your children is the most expensive gift you can give them. However, the ramifications of your investment will be priceless.

How many times have you heard a more "mature" mother say, "Cherish this time with your kids because it will be gone before you know it. They grow up so fast!" During this season of your life, when your children are still young, you will no doubt sacrifice many opportunities for yourself in order to soak up every opportunity to enjoy the childhood years which will one day be gone forever. You may decide to romp at Silver Lake Park instead of joining an aerobics class or play Candy Land for the umpteenth time on Family Game Night rather than going to a movie with the girls. I assure you that when our children have left home, none of us will lament that we wish we "hadn't spent so much time with our kids."

This chapter is intended to provide you with lots of ideas for activities you may enjoy doing at home. None of these activities require much preparation or money.

Cook with Your Kids

My son, Ben, is four and absolutely loves to cook with me. It has become our special thing to do together. I can hardly make toast without him pulling up a chair imploring, "I do it! I do it!" We have been able to work on speech and language skills, counting, and fine motor skills in a really fun way. Even more importantly, we are building a relationship that will be the basis for a lifelong friendship. There are some great cookbooks available that are designed with children in mind. We have occasionally used these resources but, more often I find that special recipes and cookbooks are not necessary to enjoy cooking with children. Almost any recipe I tackle can include little hands to help count eggs, dump ingredients, and stir. Some of our favorite treats are:

Smoothies

- ½ package frozen strawberries
- 2 bananas
- 16 ounces vanilla yogurt

Combine in a blender or smoothie machine and blend until smooth.

Snicker/Chocolate Chip Cookies

- 2 tubes refrigerator chocolate chip cookie dough
- 1 bag Snickers bite size candy bars

Cut dough into slices and wrap each slice around a bite size Snicker. Bake according to the cookie dough instructions on the package. Try different cookie dough and candy variations! We have also enjoyed peanut butter cookies with chocolate-caramel Rolo candies.

G.O.R.P.

(Good Old Raisins and Peanuts)

Choose any of the following ingredients to use. The number of ingredients and the quantity of each will determine the size of your batch.

- Raisins
- Peanuts (salted or dry roasted)
- Chex Cereal (rice, corn, wheat, or mixed)
- M & Ms
- Dried fruit bits
- Sunflower kernels
- Granola
- Pretzels
- Cheerios
- Goldfish Crackers
- Chocolate chips

Measure equals amounts of your chosen ingredients into a Ziploc bag, seal it, and shake it until well mixed.

I remember cooking with my mom, using my Junior Better Homes and Gardens Cookbook. There is a new version now; Better Homes and Gardens New Junior Cookbook. Other good children's cookbooks include:

- Silly Snacks (Better Homes and Gardens Test Kitchen) by Jennifer Darling (Editor),

- There's a Chef in My Soup! Recipes for the Kid in Everyone by Emeril Lagasse

- Kids Cook!: Fabulous Food for the Whole Family (Williamson Kids Can! Series) by Sarah Williamson

- Children's Step-by-Step Cookbook by Angela Wilkes

- Children's Quick And Easy Cookbook by Angela Wilkes

Get Dirty with Your Kids

Kids love to get dirty and it's good for them too. When you don't worry about the mess and you let your kids enjoy some of these sensory experiences, they learn about textures, smells, creativity, responsibility, problem solving, and most importantly, they have fun.

*The following recipes have been collected over many years. I made one of the playdough recipes when I was a little girl. I have cut recipes out of the Post Bulletin, surfed the Internet, ripped them out of parenting magazines, and copied them from friends. While I am unable to give credit to the source of each recipe, I want to thank those who have willingly shared their tried and true favorites. I hope that you enjoy making these with your children. I encourage you to add your favorites to these pages too. Remember that you and your children are only limited by your own imagination!

DOUGHY FUN

Kool-Aid Playdough

(Vicki's favorite)

- 1 cup flour
- ¼ cup salt
- 2 tablespoons cream of tartar
- 1 envelope unsweetened Kool-Aid
- 1 cup water
- 1 tablespoon vegetable oil

In a saucepan, mix flour, salt, cream of tartar, and Kool-Aid. Stir in water and oil. Stir over medium heat 3-5 minutes or until it forms a ball. Don't add flour. It will thicken and become smoother as it cools. When cool enough to handle, knead dough. Store in a Ziploc bag in the refrigerator.

*Surprisingly, this playdough doesn't stain and the kids love the fact that it smells like their favorite sweet drink.

Chocolate Playdough

NOT EDIBLE!

- 2 cups flour
- 1 cup salt
- 2 cups water
- 2 tablespoons cream of tartar
- 2 tablespoons vegetable oil
- Cocoa

In a saucepan mix flour, salt, water, tartar, and oil until smooth. Cook over medium heat stirring constantly until the mixture thickens and sticks to the spoon. Cool. Knead in cocoa to desired color and aroma. Kids can set up a "chocolate factory" as they roll play- dough into different shapes and candy. They'll also enjoy using empty valentine candy boxes and filling up the papers with pretend chocolates!

Cookless Playdough

- 2 ½ cups flour
- ½ cup salt
- 1 tablespoon alum (found with the spices at your grocery store)

Mix all three dry ingredients. To this dry mixture, add 2 cups boiling water colored with food coloring. Stir until cool. Knead in 3 tablespoons vegetable oil and scent, if desired. This keeps well if it's stored tightly.

Toddler Mud

- 4 rolls toilet paper
- 3 cups Ivory Snow (or liquid hand soap)
- 1 gallon warm water

Let kids help unroll the toilet paper. Mix soap and water together in a bucket. Add toilet paper and allow paper to absorb the soap mixture. Store in an empty 5-quart ice cream bucket with a lid. Play with "mud" in shallow dishpans placed on a plastic tablecloth on the floor or make this in the summer and enjoy it in the driveway. This will keep at least one month.

Oogly

- 1 box cornstarch
- 2 cups water

In a large bowl, mix ingredients. The mix will appear liquid, but when you squeeze it, it will form a ball and them become liquid again once the pressure is released. The consistency should be at a peculiar state of not quite liquid and not quite solid. If you provide bowls, slotted and solid spoons, sieves, bowls and spatulas as play props, your kids will have tons of fun. Clean up is easy. After the water dries up all that's left is dry powder.

Fruity Putty

- 3 ounces sugar-free flavored Jell-O
- 2 cups flour
- 1 cup salt
- 4 tablespoons cream of tartar
- 2 cups boiling water
- 2 tablespoons vegetable oil

Mix the dry ingredients in a saucepan. Add the boiling water and oil. Stir over medium heat until mixture forms a ball. Dump on waxed paper, cool slightly and knead. Kids love the unique texture and intense aroma, much like the chocolate playdough.

Silly Slime

- *1 cup liquid starch*
- *1 cup Elmer's glue*
- *A few drops of food coloring*

Mix ingredients together until it forms a ball. If the mixture is too sticky, add a little more starch.   Parents may not have any idea what to do with this slimy stuff, but believe me, if you put it in the hands of children, they will have a great time experiencing this new tactile sensation and will have lots of creative uses for it.

Flubber

- *2 tablespoons Borax (found in the laundry aisle at the grocery store)*
- *1/3 cup Elmer's glue*
- *Food coloring*
- *1/3 cup water plus additional 1/3 cup water (divided)*
- *One large plastic jar with a screw on lid*
- *One empty cup*

Step 1:

Add together: Elmer's glue

1/3 cup water

Food coloring

Shake, stir or mix these ingredients until glue dissolves in water

Step 2:

Fill an empty cup with 1/3 cup of water. Slowly pour in Borax; allow to settle for a minute. Pour off excess water and discard the water.

Step 3:

Scrape the wet Borax from step 2 into the jar with mix from step 1 and close the lid. Shake vigorously until the Flubber solidifies and the sides of the jar look clean.

GAK

(This is similar to Nickelodeon's "GAK")

- 2 cups white glue
- 1 1/2 cups water at room temperature
- 1 cup hot water
- 2 1/2 tablespoons Borax

Thoroughly blend glue and room temperature water. In larger bowl, combine hot water and Borax, stirring until Borax is dissolved. Slowly pour glue mixture into Borax mixture, stirring constantly. Turn out and knead until it is no longer sticky. Keeps for weeks in a tightly covered container in the fridge.

- GAK is similar to silly putty. You can make it white and the kids can color it with markers. When colored with markers, it quickly turns slate-gray/brown, but it's cheap and easy to make another batch. You can also color it with food coloring or cut it with scissors.

Salt Dough

- *2 cups flour*
- *1 cup salt*
- *1/2 - 3/4 cup water*

Mix the salt into the flour and add the water slowly as you mix. Add as much water as it takes to have a "dough-like" consistency. You can air dry this salt dough overnight for thinner items, or over a few days for larger projects. For oven drying, bake it dry at 300 degrees F. for 2-3 hours or longer depending on the thickness of the piece.

Once dry, you can paint it using watercolors, temperas, or acrylics.

CREATIVITY WITH COLOR

Sidewalk Chalk

- 1 cup plaster of paris
- 1 cup water
- Powdered tempera paint

Mix the plaster of paris and the water. For colored chalk, add powdered tempera paint in desired color. Let mixture stand for a few minutes and then pour into mold (toilet paper rolls work well). Dry completely; at least 24 hours.

Bath Paint

- 2 tablespoons liquid soap
- Food coloring

Portion the soap into several containers and add food coloring to make paint shades. Let kids paint the tub and themselves as they bathe. These paints rinse easily off the children, the tub, the walls and you!

Soap Crayons for the Bathtub

- 1 3/4 cup Ivory Snow flakes
- 50 drops food coloring
- 1/4 cup water

Mix water and soap flakes together. Add food coloring and put mixture into an ice cube tray. Allow hardening. Break or cut into pieces. Fun to write with on the tub when bathing and on face and hands! These also work on paper.

Snow Paint

- Food coloring
- Water

Place water and food coloring in empty spray bottle. Let children spray colors on the snow to make designs.

Crayons

- Broken crayon pieces
- Muffin tin, candy mold or cupcake pan

Place crayon pieces into muffin tin, candy mold or cupcake pan. Keep your colors together (i.e. browns w/brown, purples w/purples, etc.). Heat the oven to 400 degrees. Leave crayons in the oven long enough to melt. Turn off the oven and the crayons in the oven until cooled or take them out very carefully so as not to mix colors. Wax will be very hot. Allow crayons to cool completely (approximately 30 minutes) before using them.

Finger Paint

- 1 cup cornstarch
- 4 cups water
- 1/3 cup sugar

Cook in the microwave until thick. Divide into containers and tint with food coloring. Use directly on the tabletop and lift off paint with paper when child is finished.

Kool-aid Finger Paint

- *2 cups flour*
- *2 packs unsweetened Kool-aid*
- *1/2 cup salt*
- *3 cups boiling water*
- *3 tablespoon oil*

Mix the dry ingredients in a bowl. Add water and oil, stir. Use glossy finger paint paper sprayed with a bit of water.

MISCELANEOUS SENSORY FUN

Bubbles

- *5 cups cold water*
- *½ cup Joy or Dawn dish detergent*
- *2 tablespoons glycerin (available at a pharmacy)*

Measure ingredients carefully and gently mix together in a large container. The longer the solution sits, the better it gets.

Sleepy-Time Bottle

- Clear plastic bottle
- Clear corn syrup
- Glitter and/or sequins
- Food coloring, if desired

Put 1/3 cup of corn syrup into the empty plastic bottle. Add food coloring, if desired. Next, add a small amount of glitter and/or sequins. Glue on the cover. These bottles are relaxing and good to use at nap time for children who have a hard time settling down. Babies enjoy rolling these bottles around on the floor or turning them around and around and watching the thick gel flow and slosh in the bottle. It's mesmerizing.

Recipe for Faux Snow

With an electric mixer beat white powdered laundry soap with cold water. Add water gradually to produce a substance that holds together, is not runny, and can pack like a snowball. Use to model snowmen. Add twigs for arms, dried peas for eyes and mouth, thick yarn for a scarf, tiny carrot end, or orange pipe cleaner bit for a nose, acorn top cap. Sprinkle with clear glitter for sparkle.

To Dye For

Dyed Macaroni for necklaces

or

Dyed rice for a Tactile Tub

- 1 pint Pasta or Rice
- 2 teaspoon food coloring
- 3 teaspoon rubbing alcohol

Place the object to be dyed into a gallon-size ziploc bag. Add rubbing alcohol and food color. Zip it up and shake slowly, making sure you cover all the pasta with color. Spread out on layers of cookie sheets in a single layer to dry. Allow drying for several hours.

My kids have loved stringing necklaces out of dyed pasta or drawing pictures or practicing letters on cookie sheets filled with dyed rice.

Create Centers with Your Kids

At some point the Playdough, Legos, and dollhouse pieces took over our home. It was then that I took control and bought several clear plastic tubs with lids. Because they are clear I don't need to label them and am able to tell the contents of each box at a glance. Each box is the equivalent of two shoeboxes and they stack on top of each other nicely. Now I have packed up all of these little toys, stored them in the clear tubs, and have put them away in a closet to be pulled out occasionally as a special "center." Mind you, I choose not to let my children have free access to these centers. We decide together which center will come out of storage each day and I get the center out. When we are finished we work together to clean up the center and pack it away. It will come as no surprise to you, I'm sure, that these centers are played with much more often than the toys were when they were always available. These are some of the centers we have created:

- **Playdough**

  This tub only stores the utensils used to play with the Playdough. It includes rolling pins, cookie cutters, lids, spoons, Popsicle sticks, and some store-bought Playdough-brand tools. Dollar stores are often a great place to find inexpensive playdough tools.

- **Pasta/Rice**

  Buy generic pasta of different shapes and dump it into a tub with spoons and little containers. My kids often end up digging into the Tupperware cupboard and gathering various bowls with lids to concoct grand creations. Check out the recipe for dying pasta and rice.

- **Matching Game**

  Save those lids from your frozen juice cans until you have about 20 - 24 of them. Find stickers with simple and recognizable objects, like teddy bears, smiley faces, etc... Make sure you have two identical stickers of each object. Put a sticker on each of the lids. Spread them upside down on the floor and turn them over one at a time, and have your toddler try to remember where the matching object is. For younger toddlers, turn them right side up and have the child find the matching objects. Even babies like to play with the lids, and look at the objects or listen to them "clink" together. This is safe, inexpensive and provides lots of fun and learning for your child.

- **Shake, Rattle & Roll!**

  Make fun and inexpensive rattles for your baby or toddler by using plastic containers you have at home. Plastic soda bottles, yogurt containers and frosting tubs are just some examples of the containers you can use. Fill with popcorn seeds, dried beans, pennies, or anything else that makes an interesting sound when you shake it. Decorate the containers with stickers, cutouts, or decorative contact paper. Make sure that the container is taped or glued securely before giving it to a child.

- **Small Toys**

  You know all of those small toys that you always step on, your children haul in their Tonka dump trucks, and you never see them play with them as they were intended? Those toys can go into centers. We have small tubs for matchbox cars, Legos, and doll house pieces. When these toys are "resurrected" every few weeks, the kids are much more excited to play with them and their creativity abounds.

- **Craft Box**

  The sky is the limit for this tub. We have lots of the following supplies in our tub: construction paper, scissors, glue sticks, markers, crayons, stickers, stamps, sequins, ric-rac, paint, pipe cleaners, pom-poms, etc. One thing that has been a lifesaver is our Cool Whip container full of torn up construction paper. The kids enjoyed ripping various pieces of colored paper into pieces 1-2 inches in size. Then they use glue sticks to attach them to a large sheet of paper and create pictures. What you choose to include in this tub will be determined by the ages of the children who will enjoy using it. Consider including plastic scissors, round tipped scissors, or no scissors at all, if your children are under 3 years of age. Certainly supervise the use of tools of this nature. Washable markers, crayons, and glue can all be found at discount stores. This box can grow with your children as you add smaller, messier, and sharper items as they mature.

Use your Imagination and be Creative with Your Kids

In Minnesota there are plenty of days when going outside isn't an option and only indoor fun will do. On other days it's possible to be outside all day long without a care in the world. Having lots of ideas of things to do both inside and outside can make a stay-at-home mom's life infinitely easier!

- Indoor Tents

    Indoor tents are a rainy day favorite! (Or when the kids are driving you mad and you have something you want to get done!) You can erect tents pretty much anywhere, but my favorite spot that amuses them for hours, with no worries of toppling chairs, is the kitchen table. Temporarily relocate your kitchen chairs. Take one or two large sheets or blankets and cover the longest ends of the table, essentially making it a fort or tunnel! Take care to check underneath the table for any metal connecting which need to be covered. I use a small

piece of Styrofoam and some packing tape to permanently
cover those pieces. Indoor tents provide hours of fun!

- **Have a Wet & Wild Day**

  Plan this event at least a week in advance. Encourage each
  child to invite some friends over for a "Splash Day". On the
  Splash day, set up a sprinkler, a water slide (the yellow slides
  you can buy inexpensively at your local discount store -usually
  around $10), a kiddie pool, some water guns, water balloons
  and some lawn chairs. Your children will have a blast while you
  lay out and get a nice tan! For a special treat serve
  homemade juice popsicles and Kool-aid.

- **Go to the dollar store.**

  Give your children each one or two dollars to spend on
  anything they want. Plus they can use their own money for
  any extra items they want.

- **Have a movie night.**

  Kids like to pretend they are at the movie theater. Make your
  own homemade tickets and use play money. Then make some

popcorn. Assign children jobs such as usher, ticket taker, and concessions clerk. You can either rent a movie or put on a favorite video you already own. We actually get most of our movies from the Public Library. They have an awesome selection including new releases.

We do this every Friday night as we recover from our week at school and work. Our tradition also includes ordering out for pizza and eating it on the floor picnic-style as we sit on a vinyl tablecloth or a Neat Sheet.

- **Go to the park & have a picnic.**
  Prepare sandwiches and juice boxes and place them in a picnic basket. Be sure to bring an old tablecloth along. Pick a park with a swing set and play equipment. See our list of parks in the "Free Things to Do in Rochester" chapter.

- **Play dress up.**
  Get out the old clothes from the attic and allow the kids to have fun dressing up! For added fun - use face paint too. Garage sales and Good Will are other good resources for

dress up clothes. We have also waited until the week after Halloween and purchased costumes for nearly nothing. Most discount stores will have costumes, as well as some grocery stores, craft/fabric stores and the Disney Store (686 Apache Mall). One year we gave several costumes to our daughter for Christmas. She loved them! Buy these costumes as large as you can so that they fit for a few years and a few kids. Also, talk to friends. We have inherited dental hygienist smocks, graduate gowns, and old hats, shoes, and purses from friends.

Other Fun Cures for "I am BORED" Syndrome

- Read books

- Blow bubbles

- Draw

- Color

- Paint

- Use binoculars

- Use a magnifying glass

- Experiment with magnets

- Surprise a neighbor with a good deed

- Have a Teddy Bear Picnic

- Chase butterflies

- Plant a Pizza Pot – Vegetables and herbs planted in a barrel can later become pizza

- Make homemade wrapping paper or gift cards with stamps

- Play in the sandbox

- Fold laundry (O.K., I just had to throw that in there. It was worth a try!)

- Finger paint with pudding

- Paint the sidewalk with water

- Start a summer journal
- Have neighborhood bike wash
- Look at scrapbooks or organize your photo albums
- Play hide-and-seek
- Create a symphony with bottles of water or with pots and pans
- String noodles or cereal to make a necklace
- Spill food near an ant hill and watch what happens
- Cut pictures out of old magazines and make a collage
- Finger-paint with shaving cream
- Bake cookies
- Take a nap in the shade of a tree

Free Things to Do in

Rochester

"My God shall supply all your need

according to his riches in glory

by Christ Jesus."

Phillipians 4:19

I discovered when my son was nine months old that he loved

watching large equipment such as bulldozers and diggers at work. I

have never taken the time to actually see how the machines work or what they do. Children see things that we become too busy to notice. It brings entertainment at no cost, and I don't have to do any work but drive to a site and talk about what is being built. I like these types of activities.

Literature and Story Hours

Rochester Public Library	Adult section: 285-8000
	101 2nd Street SE
	Children's section: 285-8012
	www.rochesterpubliclibrary.com

The library is a great place to spend a morning with your children. The children's section is designed for little bodies with small tables and chairs and comfy couches to snuggle up with a good book. The adult sections are located on the first and second levels.

Children's section includes age-appropriate books, magazine, videos, and computer programs.

Other activities:

* Reading programs with rewards during school year and

* Book Mobile travels to neighborhoods (call for locations)

* Evening bedtime story time - Tuesdays at 7:00 p.m.

* Daytime story hour for three years to school-age on

Wednesday a.m. and Thursday a.m. in the auditorium.

Puppet shows, movies, and flannel boards are used to

assist in telling the stories. Inquire at the children's

desk for sign-up information.

Adult section has books on tape, videos and DVDs and music

CDs.

New books to rent for $2

* Upstairs is reference area, magazines (all popular titles)

You can look up information of interest from a home

computer. You can reserve from there, too, and the library

calls you when material comes in; you can renew books

online

Barnes & Noble Story Hour

Children in strollers all the way up to kindergarten age will enjoy

listening to the gifted storytellers at Barnes & Noble. Enjoy

singing, listening to stories, and on occasion sharing a cookie

with a favorite character from a book all in the children's section.

Parents should stay with their children during the 30 minute story time. Come early to get a front-row seat-it fills up fast!

Apache Mall Location

Monday and Wednesday at 11:00 a.m. in the

children's section

* Thomas the Train table for kids to play with while

parents browse

281-7950   1201 12th Street SW

Galleria Mall Location

Friday at 10:00 a.m. in the

down stairs children's section

288-3848 15 1st Street SW downtown Rochester

Movies/Arts

The Chateau Theatres   536-7469

3450 East Circle Drive NE

www.chateautheatres.com

ROCHESTER'S #1 MOVIE THEATRE

* FREE "Kids Show" offered every Saturday morning at 10:30am. doors open at 9:30 am for games, contests and prizes prior to the scheduled movie.
* "REEL BABIES" a program (1st and the 3rd Tuesday mornings of each month) designed for parents with infants & babies not yet walking. Enjoy a current release at a matinee price in a "baby friendly" theater, complete with comfortable rocking chairs, changing stations, breast feeding areas. Our friendly staff will even deliver your lunch to you!
* FREE Easter Bunny pictures & Egg Hunt
* FREE Halloween Party & Movie (safe alternative to "Trick or Treating" or nasty weather)
* FREE pictures with Santa
* Fun Birthday Party Packages
* eTicketing
* End of School Year Parties
* Back to School Bash
* Non Profit Ticket Programs ideal for schools & organizations
* Auditorium Rentals *Food Court

Children's Dance Theatre   281-2810

P.O. Box 6655

Young dancers perform in professional productions. Productions are geared for elementary-aged children. Call for a schedule of performances.

The Masque Youth Theatre and School

287-0704

14 4th Street SW

www.masque.org

Present a variety of family entertainment including five main stage productions, puppet shows, and education programs for all ages.

The Rochester Art Center   282-8629

40 Civic Center Drive SE

www.rochesterartcenter.org

This is a place for the entire family to enjoy a day together. The Art Center offers Family Free Days the third Sunday of each month throughout the summer. Families can participate in hands-on activities that are related to that month's exhibit. Free on Thursdays. Adult admission: $3, Seniors $2, students and members free.

Nature Parks

What a great way for your family to spend time outdoors playing, eating, and enjoying the fresh air. Rochester has a fantastic park system with locations close to any neighborhood and some right in your own backyard!

Quarry Hill Nature Center   281-6114

701 Silver Creek Rd. NE

*Nature building with native animals, fish, and reptiles on display. Paved trails, nature ponds, and hiking trails to caves.

Directions: coming from the north, take East Circle Drive, past Viola Rd. stop lights, then the turn right at Silver Creek Rd. Coming from the south, take Hwy. 14 East and turn left at stop lights (30th Avenue SE), proceed to go past stop lights at

College View Rd. SE and turn left at Silver Creek Rd.

Hours: Nature Building-Monday - Friday 9:00 a.m. - 5:00 p.m.

Saturday 12:00 - 5:00 p.m.

Chester Woods Park   287-2624

8378 Highway 14 East, Eyota, MN

*This park features hiking trails and a lake with a beach and

swimming area-no lifeguard on duty.

Directions: Take Hwy. 14 east 7 miles past Rochester.

Oxbow Park and Zollman Zoo 775-2451

5731 County Rd. 105 NW,

Byron, MN

*The zoo offers educational programs regarding Minnesota

wild life. There are picnic areas and hiking trails to explore as well.

Directions: Take Hwy. 14 west to Byron (about 5 miles), turn

right at stop lights by Kwik Trip, go straight until sign for Oxbow located on right side, follow arrows.

Hours: Park is open from 7:00 a.m. - 10:00 p.m.

Zoo Summer hours: 12:00 p.m. - 4:00 p.m.

Winter hours: 12:00 p.m. - 4:00 p.m.

City Parks and Playgrounds in Rochester

We are lucky to have plenty of great parks here in Rochester. In every neighborhood there is a playground within walking distance that provides many hours of entertainment. What you look for in a park depends on your interests and the ages of your children. Have you ever pulled up next to a park assuming they have at least water? I now carry a "park kit" in my car. My "park kit" includes:

-a wide plastic hamper

-sand toys

-balls

-bubbles

-Frisbees

-a baseball mitt

- mesh bag

-extra change of clothes for each child

-hats

-sun screens

-lip balm

-a disposable camera

-snacks

-small first aid kit

-hand sanitizer

-wet wipes

-plastic sack(a place for wet/soiled items)

-a blanket or reusable/beach mat and towel to
  wipe off the morning dew

*an insulated cooler:

-partially filled and frozen water bottles (make

  -Sippy cups

  -juice boxes

  -fruit

  -perishable items

Time saving tips for keeping the car organized and ready for running errands:

Small basket:

-place items to be returned

-kid's compact discs/praise music

-tissue

-personal toiletries

Organizers that fit over back seat:

-small toys

-wet wipes,

-diapers

-Sippy cups

-other treasures

*Inexpensive organizers can be found at discount stores in automotive or baby departments, home stores such as Bed, Bath and Beyond.

*Neat Sheets-big, blue waterproof blankets. These are great for kids to eat on while traveling and for impromptu picnics. They also make a wonderful, outdoor play mat. These are available at most discount stores.

We have visited each park listed with playground equipment. In our opinion, we listed appropriate ages that would benefit from the park. Please use your own discretion for safety. It took us a total of 10 hours to visit all of the parks, but what an educational and eye-opening experience for us! We also traveled to parts of Rochester that we don't frequent due to distance, but we both agreed there are parks we will return to this summer.

According to information provided by Rochester Parks and Recreation department, 281-6160, the following parks have shelters, requiring reservations for large groups:

Bear Creek

Central

Cook

East Park

Eastwood

Essex

Foster-Arend

Kutzky

Quarry Hill

East and West Silver Lake

Slatterly

Soldier's Field

Three Links at Silver Lake

The shelters have restrooms and electricity. Call Park and Recreation for reservation and fees.

Check the City of Rochester Website for more information and details on facility rentals.

www.rochestermn.gov

NORTHWEST

Location	FOR 1-3 YEAR OLDS	FOR 3-5 YEAR OLDS	FOR 5-12 YEAR OLDS	YEAR EQUIPMENT TO BE REPLACED	YEAR EQUIPMENT NEW	TYPE OF EQUIPMENT	SHELTER	SHADE	RESTROOMS	ON-SITE PARKING	DRINKING WATER	PICNIC TBLS & BENCHES
Allendale-3000 Block of 18th Ave. NW	X	X	X	2015	2000	P		X		X		X
Arborglen-31 Ave. & Arbor Dr. NW	X	X	X	2010	92/01	P						X
Cimarron-48th St. & 20 1/2 th Ave. NW	X	X	X	2018	2003	P						X
John R. Cooke-7th St. & 7th Ave. NW	X	X	X	2012	1997	P		X	X	X	X	X
Crescent-28th St. & 15th Ave. NW	X	X	X	2014	99/01	P	X		X	X	X	X
Diamond Ridge-46th Ave. & Valley Dr. NW	X	X	X	2010	1995	P						X
Elton Hills-13th Ave. & 22nd St. NW	X	X	X	2013	1998	P		X	X	X	X	
Essex Park-West River Rd. (sign)	X	X	X	2018	2003	P						X
Essex West-5455 West River Rd. NW	X	X	X	2014	1999	P	X	X	X	X	X	X
Foster Arend-37th St. & E. River Rd		X	X	00/15	85/02	P		X				X
Goose Egg-9th St. & 2nd Ave. NW	X	X	X	2016	87/01	P						X
E. Starr Judd-3rd St. & 36th Ave. NW	X	X	X	2013	1988	M						

Park											
Kings Run-50th St. & 18th Ave. NW	X					P	1992	2007	X	X	X
Kutzky-2nd St. & 13th Ave. NW	X	X	X	X	X	P	85/00	2015	X	X	X
Manor-3rd St. & 42nd Ave. NW	X		X	X		P	2003	2018	X	X	X
Nachreiner-22nd St. & 25th Ave. NW	X			X		M	1995	2010		X	X
North Park-Fairway Dr. & 44th St. NW	X				X	W	1991	2006			X
Rolling Green-38th St. & 21st Ave. NW					X	P	79/98	2013	X	X	X
Schmidt-63rd St. & 24th Ave. NW	X					P	1991	2006	X	X	X
Viking-26th St. & 2nd Ave. NW		X	X			M	1998	2013			X
Watson Sports Complex-41st St. & W. River Rd	X	X	X			P	1992	2007	X	X	X
Wedgewood-5117 52nd Ave. NW	X					P	2000	2015	X	X	X
West Zumbro Tot Lot-1st St. & 19th Ave. NW	X			X		P			X	X	X
White Oaks-4500 block of 55th St. NW	X	X	X	X	X	P	2010	2010	X	X	X

NORTHEAST

Location	FOR 1-3 YEAR OLDS	FOR 3-5 YEAR OLDS	FOR 5-12 YEAR OLDS	YEAR EQUIPMENT NEW	YR EQPMT REPLACED	TYPE OF EQUIPMENT	SHELTER	SHADE	RESTROOMS	ON-SITE PARKING	DRINKING WATER	PICNIC TBLS & BENCHES
Century Hills-3100 block & 21st St. NE	×	×	×	2003	2018	P						×
East Park- E. Center & 15th Ave. NE		×	×	1988	2003	W	×			×		×
Emerald Hills-2600 Block Cassidy Dr. NE	×	×	×			P						×
Northern Hgts E-Viola Hgts Rd & Nor. Valley Dr. NE	×	×	×	1992	2007	P						×
Northern Slopes-30th St. & 6th Ave. NE		×	×	1989	2004	W/P						×
Parkwood Hills-22nd Ave. & Parkwood Hills Dr. NE	×	×	×	1994	2009	W						×
Quarry Hill-9th St. & 19th Ave. NE	×	×	×	1994	2009	M/P	×	×		×		
Sertoma Squ.-Silver Lake Dr. NE		×	×	1981	1996	W	×	×				×
Silver Lake East-7th St. & 2nd Ave. NE		×	×	1981	1996	W	×	×	×	×		×
Silver Lake West-Silver Lake Dr. NE		×	×	1997	2012	W		×	×	×		×
Three Links@Silver Lake-7th St. & 11th Ave. NE	×	×	×	96/99	2011	P	×	×	×	×	×	×
Viking Hills-Whiting Lane NE	×	×	×	1999	2014	P						×

SOUTHWEST

Location										
Baihly Hgts. Tot Lot-21st St. & Folwell Dr. SW	X			X	P	1991	2006	X	X	X
Baihly Meadows-Baihly Hills Dr. & Fox Valley Dr. SW	X			X	P	1992	2007	X	X	X
Bamber Ridge-36th St. & Halling Place SW	X				P	1992	2007	X	X	X
Eagle Ridge-4th St. & Aspen Lane SW	X		X	X	P	1997	2012	X	X	X
Elmcroft-25th St. & Oakridge Ave. SW	X		X		P	1992	2007		X	X
Fox Valley-Cty Rd. 22 & Fox Valley Rd. SW	X				P	1991	2006		X	X
Greystone-Greystone Ln. & Sherburn Pl. SW	X				P	2003	2018	X	X	X
Mohn-Country Club Rd. & Avalon Cove SW	X				P	2003	2018	X	X	X
St. Mary's-4th St. & 9th Ave. SW	X	X			P	1996	2011	X	X	X
Soldier's Mem. Field-244 E. Soldier's Field Dr. SW	X	X	X		M	1986	2001		X	X
Southern Hills-1126 Southern Hills Ln. SW	X				P	1999	2014	X	X	X
South Pointe-6220 South Pointe Dr. SW	X				P	2000	2015	X	X	X
Southern Woods-11th Ave. SW & Willow Golf Course	X		X		P	2002	2017		X	X
Younge-Fox Valley Dr. & 23rd Ave. SW	X		X		W	1994	2009	X	X	X

SOUTHEAST

Location	FOR 5-12 YEAR OLDS	FOR 3-5 YEAR OLDS	FOR 1-3 YEAR OLDS	YR EQPMT REPLACED	YEAR EQUIPMENT NEW	TYPE OF EQUIPMENT	SHELTER	SHADE	RESTROOMS	ON-SITE PARKING	DRINKING WATER	PICNIC TBLS & BENCHES
Bear Creek-Hwy 14 E. & Marion Rd. SE	X	X	X	2010	1995	P	X		X	X	X	X
Eastwood-Hwy 14 East	X	X	X	13/15	98/00	P	X	X		X		X
Friendship Tot Lot-14th St. & 4th Ave. SE	X	X	X	2018	2003	P						X
Homestead-8 1/2 St. & 15th Ave. SE	X	X		2002	1987	M						X
Mayo Memorial-E. Center St. & Civic Center Dr. SE	X	X		2001	1986	W						
McQuillan-1655 Marion Rd. SE	X	X	X	2011	1996	P			X	X	X	X
Meadow-20th St. & 5th Ave. SE	X			1999	1979	M						X
Meadow Park Estates-16th St. & 11th Ave. SE	X	X	X	2005	1990	P	X		X	X	X	
Slatterly-10th St. & 11th Ave. SE	X	X	X	2013	1998	P						X
Smetka-11th Ave. & Pinewood Rd. SE	X	X	X	2008	1994	P						X

Type of Equipment Key: M (metal), P (plastic), W (wood)

Many thanks go out to Denny Stotz, assistant superintendent of Rochester Park and Recreation Department. He was very supportive in providing us with park names, maps, and information about playground equipment.

Walking/Bike Trails

*Rochester has a superb walking/bike trail system throughout the city that includes 28.9 miles of paved, off-road bike trails.

For a map call Park & Recreation at **281-6160** or look in front of a current phone book.   **www.ci.rochester.mn.us/park**

Apache Mall   **288-8056**

*The mall encourages the hallways for walkers to use before and during mall hours. At the service desk in front of Herberger's store are maps and walking information including a walking club you may join.

Walking Hours: Monday - Saturday 7:00 a.m. - 9:00 p.m.,

Sunday 7:00 a.m. - 6:00 p.m.

Community Education/Local Schools   285-8646

*Community Education offers several local elementary and secondary schools as walking sites either before or after school. Walkers must sign up through Community Education and pay the small fee to take advantage of this program. Walking times vary at each school and are only offered during the school year.

Local Discoveries

You can either walk or drive to many places in Rochester exploring and making discoveries along the way.

* Visit a local garden nursery

Nurseries are fascinating places for children. My son watered the plants at 20 months of age. Garten Marketplatz is so enchanting that you may want to bring a sack lunch and spend a couple hours just enjoying the beautiful grounds.

Sargent's on 2ⁿᵈ Garden Center: 1811 2ⁿᵈ Street SW

289-6068

Sargent's Landscape Nursery: 7955 18ᵗʰ Avenue NW

289-0022

Jim Whiting Nursery and Garden Center:

3430 19th Street NW

289-3741

Garten Marketplatz Perennial Farms:

Salem Road SE (past Historical Society) and County Rd. 15 (Sign on right side of road), then 3 miles   281-1023

* Visit local art galleries (good idea for ages five on up) and discuss what types of art appeal to you.

Gilded Star Gallery: 324 S. Broadway

535-7572

Herring Art and Frame: 5500 Hwy. 63 South

288-4439

Fast Frame Gallery: 324 First Ave SW

287-8488

Rochester Art Center: 40 Civic Center Drive

282-8629

SE MN Visual Arts: 16 First St SW

281-4920

University Center Rochester: 855 30th Ave SE

280-2828

*The Plummer House of Arts designed by Dr. Henry S. Plummer of Mayo Clinic. The gardens are wonderful to wander through and provide a great background for picture taking. At certain times the facility is open for public viewing. The park is free.

Plummer House: 1091 Plummer Lane SW

281-6160

*Explore the skyway system of downtown Rochester. Located in the skyway between the Radisson parking ramp and the Galleria Mall local art work by students is displayed in cases. The skyway connects office buildings, medical buildings, hotels, shopping centers, and the library. Maps are located in the skyways as well as in the front of the phone book.

*Go underground to the subway system downtown which includes shops and eating areas connecting the downtown Mayo campus, hotels, and restaurants. Subway maps are located in the Mayo campus, skyways, and in front of local phone book.

Here is a fun game to play using the skyway and subway systems in downtown Rochester.

"Rochester Mole": Parent chooses an entrance to the downtown skyway system and tells the children the final destination. The children need to use maps to lead the parent to the final destination. Make sure you stay with your children, don't just set them loose. Then the parent chooses an entrance to the subway system and child/children need(s) to use maps to lead the parent back to the original starting point.

* The Peace Fountain located in Peace Plaza outside of Barnes & Noble. Bring a snack to share as you count the number of displayed doves. 1st Street SW and 1st Avenue SW

*Mayo Medical Center offers free informational, art and architectural tours for the general public. Tours begin at the Judd Auditorium, subway level of the Mayo building.

Mayo Medical Center: 200 First St. SW

284-2511

Informational tours and films: Mon.-Fri. 10 a.m.

Art and architecture tour: Tues.-Thurs. 1:30 p.m.

*Down by the Riverside series are free concerts located behind the Mayo Civic Center on Sunday evenings in July and August. There is a variety of musical entertainment both local and national. Music begins at 7 p.m., but come early, spread a blanket and enjoy a picnic dinner.

For a schedule contact: **1-800-657-3980**

*The History Center is home to items preserving the history of Rochester and Olmsted County. Information regarding genealogical materials are available, too.

Open Tuesday through Saturday.

Fee: Adults $4, Children 15 years and under $1.

Olmsted County History Center and Museum:

1195 West Circle Drive SW

282-9447

*Soldiers Field Veteran's Memorial honors those who died while serving in the Armed Forces. Includes a beautiful sculpture garden, wonderful art, and provides a place for children to run.

Corner of Seventh St. and Second Avenue SW

*Visit a local pet store to pet the puppies and kittens and observe the different kinds of fish in the aquariums. For a minimal cost you can feed the puppies a scoop of food. The local animal shelter will let you pet the dogs during outside exercise time.

Fish-N-Pets: 1201 Broadway S Crossroads Center

281-4461

Rochester Animal Control: 2122 Campus Drive SE

287-2230

*Save your bread crumbs for feeding the geese at Silver Lake. The geese are used to being fed and will come up very close to you. You may want to wear an old pair of shoes since the sidewalks and grass are full of goose droppings

Silver Lake Drive NE

* The Rochester airport is a fun place to visit. With heightened security you won't be able to go inside just to watch planes land and take off. It's easy to park on a road near the airport which provides a clear view of airplane traffic.

Hwy. 63 South and Airport Road

*The farmer's market is held from 7:30 a.m.-noon Saturday beginning in June and continuing through September. There are many items to choose from such as vegetables, fruits, flowers, and meats. Find ingredients to make a salad or try a new vegetable.

Located in the parking lot next to Mayo Memorial Park

4th Street and 4th Avenue SE

536-0697

*A short drive northeast of Rochester will bring you to Apple Ridge Orchards. On weekends during the Fall hay rides are provided up the hill to the orchards. Also, a corn maze, llamas, and barnyard animals are available for petting. Check for seasonal hours and times.

Apple Ridge Orchard: Mazeppa, MN 55956

(507) 843-3033

*Sekapp Orchard and Farms have strawberries, raspberries, apples and pumpkins to pick in season. Produce priced by the pound. Tours are given by appointment for a small fee. Hours open 9a.m.-7p.m., June 15-November.

Sekapp Orchard and Farms: 3415 College view Road E

(1 mile east of Rochester on County Road 9)

*Want to know how bread or bagels are made? The Bread Baker Company gives tours and free samples of the products they make. The staff is friendly and ready to answer all questions. Call to arrange a tour.

The Bread Baker Company: 16 17th Ave NW

289-7052

*Want to ice skate in July? You can skate and swim year-round at the Rochester Recreational Center. Schedule changes weekly. Call for times. Minimal fee.

Rochester Recreation Center: 21 Elton Hills Drive NW

Schedule: **287-2134**

*J.E.T.S. — USA Gymnastics and All-Star Cheerleading provides preschool open mornings and evenings and open gym for all ages on Saturday. Small fee.

J.E.T.S. Gymnastics:

4430 19th St NW

285-9262

Seasonal Discoveries

Rochester and the surrounding communities offer a variety of activities to choose from in each season.

*The Transportation Fair is sponsored by PAIIR and held annually the third Saturday in May. Kids are allowed to climb on and look at vehicles ranging from school buses to cement trucks. This event is free.

PAIIR: Northrop Education Center, 201 8th St NW

285-8033

*The Rochester Honkers, a summer, collegiate baseball league begins the season June 1 and continues through mid August. The Honkers play at Mayo Field. Ticket prices include: Adult $5, Child/Senior $3.

Rochester Honkers: 403 E. Center Street

289-1170

www.rochesterhonkers.com

*Rochesterfest an annual event held the third week in June. Many events such as concerts and hot air balloon races are free. Food vendors line up the street in front of the Mayo Civic Center. By purchasing a Rochesterfest button you receive discount admission to events and activities.

Rochesterfest: www.rochesterfest.com

*The Rochester Water Ski Club provides great entertainment. They perform free shows on Wednesday evenings at 7 p.m. at

Lake Zumbro by Fisherman's Inn. The shows last approximately 1-2 hours.

Water Ski Club Shows: 8 Fisherman Drive NW, Oronoco, MN

*The Dodge County Fair is small, but offers many fun things for preschool and school-aged children. Feast your eyes on large farm equipment, a petting zoo, pig races, and inexpensive kiddie rides. The fair is held either the second or third weekend in July. Admission is free. There is a small parking fee.

Dodge County Fair: Dodge County Fairgrounds

North Mantorville Ave, Kasson, MN

(507) 634-7736

*The Olmsted County Fair provides activities for the entire family. Each day there are free activities listed and if you arrive before noon, admission is free. Come see the different 4-H exhibits, animals, midway rides and food vendors. Admission for adults, $2, children age 6-12, $1. There is a fee for parking on the fairgrounds. The fair is held around the first week of August.

Olmsted County Fair: 16th St and 3rd Ave SE, Rochester, MN

*October brings Fire Prevention Safety Month. Fire stations in Rochester open up in the evenings to the public during a scheduled week. Information, coloring books, fire hats, and refreshments are part of this event. Kids can climb into a fire truck and staff is present to answer all questions. This event is free.

*December brings the Live Nativity. Stay warm in your car as you drive past live displays depicting events leading to Jesus' birth. This event is Friday through Sunday evenings the first weekend in December.

Crossroads College: 920 Mayowood Rd. SW

288-4563

Regional Discoveries

The entire family can spend a day visiting regional attractions and enjoying the gifts nature has to offer.

*The SPAM Museum is dedicated to the 1937 canned meat food invention. World War II soldiers overseas ate SPAM.

Fun facts and SPAM related items will entertain all ages.

Hours: Tuesday-Saturday 10 a.m.- 5 p.m.,

Sunday 12 p.m. - 4 p.m.

1937 SPAM Boulevard (north end of Main Street), Austin, MN

1-800-LUV-SPAM

*JC Hormel Nature Center provides 278 acres of forest, prairie, and streams for you to explore.

Hours: 9a.m.-12p.m. and 1p.m.-5p.m. Monday-Friday; 1p.m.-5p.m. Sunday. Walking/hiking trails open 6a.m.-10p.m. daily. Trails connect to Austin's paved, ten mile bike trail system.

1304 21st St. NE, Austin, MN

507-437-7519

*Avian Acres Wild Bird Supply is your native bird supply headquarters. Everything from bird seed to bird houses, books and candles relating to birds can be found under one roof. Bob, the store owner, encourages children as young as six years old to become involved in the life-long hobby of identifying and feeding birds. Group tours are available by appointment at no charge.

Open Tuesday-Saturday 9 a.m.- 7 p.m.

Route 2, Box 5, Lanesboro, MN

1.2 miles south of the town Lanesboro on Norway Drive.

1-800-967-2473

*Eagle Bluff Environmental Learning Center offers year-round educational and recreational opportunities. It is well-known for the outdoor ropes course and interpretive nature trails. Better for elementary age and older children.

1991 Brightsdale Road, near Lanesboro, MN

1-888-800-9558

*Lanesboro State Fish Hatchery provides information and education regarding the fish raised in this environment. Hours: Monday-Friday 7a.m.-4:30p.m.. Group tours available.

Rt. 2, Box 85, Lanesboro, MN

507-467-3771

*Wabasha's historical main street bordering the Mississippi River is a great Saturday get-a-way. The National Eagle Center provides information on bald-eagle watching. If you are lucky, you will see eagles soaring over the river. A small public library and antique shops are also on Main Street. The movie Grumpy Old Men was filmed here.

152 Main Street, Wabasha, MN

651-565-4989

*Forestville History Center provides a look at how life was for the town of Forestville during the late 1800's. Costumed actors inform visitors about each building that remains in this historic town.

Price per adult $4, children ages 6-12 years $2, under 6 years free.

Forestville State Park, Preston, MN

507-765-2785

Camping Opportunities

Camping in southeastern Minnesota provides the opportunity to get close to nature and take in the beautiful scenery of lakes, prairies, and bluffs. Providing all that and more, the following parks and campgrounds are a few of the region's biggest, and welcome campers who use everything from tents to recreational vehicles.

Albert Lea/Austin KOA Kampground

84259 County Road 46, Hayward, MN 56043

1-800-562-5196

Features: laundry, recreation room, pavilion, swimming pool, playgrounds, badminton, sports field, horseshoes, volleyball.

Beaver Trails Campground

219443 630th Avenue, Austin, MN 55912

1-800-245-6281

www.beavertrails.com

Features: breakfast with fresh-made doughnuts, free hay rides, movies, swimming, contests, kiddie train rides, mini golf, laundry, kiddie fishing pool, paddle boats, shuffleboard.

Bluff Valley Campground

RR1 Box 194 (Bluff Valley Rd), Zumbro Falls, MN 55991

(507) 263-3701, www.campbvc.com/may2003.htm

Features: Live music, karaoke, theme weekends, planned activities, inner tubing, mini golf, games, breakfast and dinner buffets, arcade, movie rentals, convenience store.

Brookside Campgrounds

52482 320th, Blooming Prairie, MN 55917

(507) 583-2979

Features: heated pool and kiddie pool, phone/modem hookups, sports field, horseshoes, volleyball.

Cannon Falls Campground

30365 Oak Lane, Cannon Falls, MN 55009

(507) 263-3145.

Features: heated pool, volleyball, horseshoes, sports field, basketball, arcade, convenience store, theme weekends, planned holiday activities, access to Cannon Valley bike trails.

Hay Creek Valley Campground

31673 Hwy. 56, Red Wing, MN 55066

(651) 388-3998 or 1-888-388-3998

Features: heated pool, store with saloon, pool tables, lunches, laundry, volleyball, horseshoes, near state forest with foot and horse trails.

Hidden Valley Campground

27173 144th Avenue Way, Welch, MN 55089

(651) 258-45650.

Features: bike trails, convenience store, games room.

Island Camping and Marina

2361 Hallquist Ave., Red Wing, MN 55066

(715) 792-2502.

Features: hot spa, store, enclosed meeting area, horseshoes, laundry, walking trails, playground, slip marina on the Mississippi and Mud Lake.

Kamp Dels

14842 Sakatah Lake Rd., Waterville, MN 55096

(507) 362-8616

www.kampdels.com

Features: Olympic-sized pool, toddler pool, water park, miniature golf, tennis courts, sand volleyball, basketball, softball field, beach, games room, a petting zoo, horseback riding, access to bike trails.

Kiesler's Campground

14360 Hwy. 14 E, Waseca, MN 56093

1-800-533-4642

www.camp@kieslers.com

Features: 48-foot-long water slide, 2,000 square foot pool and wading pool, mini golf, live bands, planned activities.

Lake Byllesby Regional Campground

   7650 Echo Point Road, Cannon Falls, MN 55009

   (507) 263-4447.

Features: beach, boat launch, sports field.

Lazy "D" Trail Rides and Campground

   18748 County Rd. 39, Altura, MN 55910

   (507) 932-3098

   www.info@lazydcampground.com

Features: swimming pool, horseback riding.

Old Barn Resort

   Route 3, Box 57, Preston, MN 55965

   1-800-552-2512 or (507) 467-2512

   www.info@barnresort.com

Features: nine hole golf course, driving range, restaurant, bar, indoor heated pool, 44-bed hostel, horseshoes, sand volleyball, basketball, game room, inner tubing on the Root River and canoe and bike rentals, access to bike trails.

Treasure Prairie Island RV Park

   5734 Sturgeon Lake Rd., Welch, MN 55089

1-800-22-7077

Features: laundry, recreation room pavilion, swimming pool, whirlpool, boating, canoeing.

Wazionja Campground

6450 120th St. NW, Pine Island, MN 55963, (507) 356-8594.

Features: recreation hall, near the Douglas bike trail, weekend activities and hay rides.

Area State Park Camping Opportunities

Call for a free guide to MN State Parks:

(651) 296-6157 or 1 -888-MINNDNR

ww.dnr.state.mn.us

Each park requires a vehicle park sticker to enter. Cost: Daily - $7, Daily Group (10 permit minimum) - $5, Annual - $25, Disabled - $12

Beaver Creek Valley - 15954 County 1, Caledonia, MN 55921

(507) 724-2107

Features: hiking, fishing, and camping year round.

Directions: From I-90 take State Hwy. 76 south for 24 miles, then take Houston County Road 1 west for 4 miles.

*Office opens April 15

*Mon.-Fri.: 9 a.m.- 3 p.m., Memorial Day-Labor Day: Fri. & Sat.: 9 a.m.- 9 p.m.

Frontenac - 29223 County 28 Blvd., Frontenac, MN 55026

(651) 345-3401

Features: camping, hiking, wildflowers in Spring through Fall

Directions: 10 miles SE of Redwing on Hwy. 61 or 5 miles NW of Lake City then 1 mile N on County Road 2

Forestville/Mystery Cave - Route 2, Box 128, Preston, MN

(507) 352-5111

Features: tours of Mystery Cave, trout streams, great hiking/horseback trails, camping, spring flowers.

Directions: located 4 miles South of State Highway 16 on Fillmore County Highway 5, then 2 miles East of Fillmore County 118.

* Office opens Mon. - Thursday: 8 a.m. - 4 p.m.

Friday: 8 a.m. - 10 p.m,

Saturday: 9 a.m. - 9 p.m.

Sunday: 9 a.m. - 6 p.m.

Nerstrand-Big Woods - 9700 170th Street East,

Nerstrand, MN 55053

(507) 333-4840

Features: camping and hiking

Directions: I-35 to State Hwy. 19 E into Northfield, South on State Hwy. 3, East on State Hwy. 246, turn right on County Road 40

*Office opens 9 a.m.- 4 p.m. daily, Memorial Day - Labor Day 9 a.m.- 9 p.m.

Rice Lake - 8485 Rose Street, Owatonna, MN 55060

(507) 455-5871

Features: camping, canoeing and bird watching

Directions: I-35 take exit 42A, follow signs to Rose Street, then East on Rose Street to park

*Office opens: no times specified

Sakatah Lake – 50499 Sakatah Lake State Park Road

Waterville, MN, 56096

(507) 362-4438

Features: camping, hiking and Maple-Basswood forests

Directions: State Hwy. 60, 1 mile east of intersection on State

Hwy. 13 & 60 at Waterville

*Office open 8:30 a.m.- 9:30 p.m. daily, weekends 10 a.m.- 2 p.m.

Whitewater - Route 1, Box 265, Altura, MN, 55910

(507) 932-3007

Features: 110 sites for tent and RV, nature programs, gift shop,
hiking/nature trails, fishing pier, swimming, dump station, flush
and pit toilets. Pets ok. A maximum stay is 14 nights.
* Open April 1 - October 31

* Mon. - Fri.: 8 a.m.- 4 p.m., Sat & Sun: 9 a.m.- 5 p.m.

Camping Web Sites

www.Camp-A-Roo.com

This website is loaded with helpful hints from what to pack to

what to expect when camping with young children. There are

games, food, and camping gear offered by this site. A great

resource to keep as one of your "favorites."

www.familycampinggear.com

This web site is a great resource for "lists" such as camping gear, first aids items, safety tips, things to do with kids, etc. I found it to be user-friendly. They suggested several books.

Gordon, Herb. *The Joy of Camping*. Burford Books, 1998.

Drake, Jane. *The Kids Campfire Book*. Kids Can Press, 1996, 1998.

Tent Camping Checklist

To make your lives easier when you tent camp be organized. In one Rubbermaid container put your tent, stakes, mallet, dustpan/whisk broom, tarp, doormat, several 33 gallon trash bags (in case it rains and you need to place items in bags to keep dry), sleeping mats, rope, buck knife and/or Leatherman tool. In another Rubbermaid container store cooking supplies, towels, water containers, lighter, matches, compass, etc. This way you can just pick up and go at a moments notice. The following are check lists to use to organize your camping equipment, find what you need to purchase, and also what to replace. You may want to laminate it and keep it in the tent box.

Camp Equipment

- Air Mattress
- Air Mattress Pump
- Axe
- Batteries
- Broom, whisk
- Bungee Cords
- Chairs, folding
- Cots
- Doormat
- Fire Extinguisher
- Fire Starters
- Flashlight
- Gloves
- Hammer
- Hatchet
- Heater, Propane Tent
- Knife, Swiss Army
- Lantern
- Pillows
- Pliers
- Ponchos/Rain Gear
- Radio
- Rope/Twine
- Sleeping Bags
- Stove, Propane Fuel
- Table, folding
- Tarps
- Tent

Camping Supplies

- Aloe
- Aluminum Foil
- Bags (white/green garbage)
- Bowl
- Burner
- Camera and Film
- Can Opener
- Cash
- Citronella Candles
- Clothes
- Clotheslines
- Clothespins
- Coffee Pot
- Cups
- Detergent
- Dish Pan
- Dish Rag
- Dish Towels
- First Aid Kit
- Fly Swatter
- Fork (long handled)
- Games
- Hotdog/Marshmallow forks
- Insect Bite Remedy
- Insect Repellent
- Jackets
- Kleenex
- Knife, large & Scissors
- Knife, paring
- Knives
- Lighter/Matches
- Napkins
- Newspaper
- Pam-nonstick spray
- Pancake turner-Teflon
- Paper Towels
- Plastic Wrap
- Plates
- Pie Irons (sandwich makers)

- Pitcher
- Pot Holders
- Pots and Pans
- Scouring Pads
- Sharpening Stone
- Sippy Cups
- Skillets
- Spoons
- Spoons, Large
- Sunscreen Lotion

- Swim Gear
- Table Cloth
- Table Cloth Clamps
- Thermal Coffee Mugs
- Toiletries
- Tongs
- Towels
- Water Container
- White Garbage Bags
- Zip Lock Bags (different sizes)

NOTES

Meal Planning

"She gets up while it is still dark; she provides food for her family

and portions for her servant girls."

Proverbs 31:15

I grew up on a family farm in southwest Minnesota. We were
meat and potato people and ate a fair amount of hotdishes! I
learned to cook while I was quite young thanks to my mom and 4-
H. I can vividly recall coming home from school in the fall at eight
or nine years of age, getting on the FM radio to my mom, who
was combining in the field, and getting directions for how to fix

dinner. As an adult my cooking and shopping was a reflection of my youth.

As a stay-at-home mom, and even when I was teaching full-time, the dinner hour used to be dreaded all day. I complained to my family of being tired of always fixing the same things and rarely getting suggestions for meals. While I have always made grocery lists, they usually consisted of things that I had run out of in the previous week, rather than a list of ingredients needed for meals in the upcoming weeks. Consequently, during the "piranha" hour when everyone seemed to want a "piece" of mom, I was often frantically trying to pull together a creative meal out of very few available ingredients. It was fairly common for me to resort to expensive pre-made meals ("just add meat") or fast-food.

Proverbs 31: 15 reminded me that providing food for my family is one of my responsibilities. The mother in Proverbs 31 "gets up while it is still dark" to do so. Now, in my experience, I only get up while it is still dark to do something if it is something that I enjoy. So I found it necessary to make meal planning and preparation enjoyable. I can honestly say that I truly enjoy planning meals for my family, grocery shopping, and cooking now. Really! We are also saving a lot of money because of the changes

I have made. The following are some of the things that have worked for me.

Plan Your Meals

Menu planning does not have to be difficult. The small investment of time involved in planning your menus can result in big money savings because you eliminate trips to the store to pick up those one or two ingredients and end up spending $50.

If this task seems daunting to you, plan to start small. In the beginning you might plan for one week at a time. My husband gets paid every two weeks on Tuesday. Conveniently, our grocery stores sales start on Wednesdays. Now I plan my menus twice a month on Tuesday and shop on Wednesday.

Begin by going through your food flyers. I have one favorite store for produce and one for everything else. I use a spiral bound notebook and on one page create two columns with one store name listed at the top of each column. Next I go through their weekly ads and list all of the things that I typically need and their sale prices. Then I can easily compare the two stores and decide which store has the better deals.   Finally, using my sale list, my pantry inventory, and my freezer inventory (see at the end of this chapter) I create my menus.

I plan these menus on my Menu Planning sheet (see at the end of the chapter). You can certainly create your own sheet and a quick perusal of the Internet will find you lots more as well. I like to use a generic sheet that I can run several copies of and just fill in the two weeks worth of dates and meals each time I plan. In each box I put the meal and the source (cookbook name, recipe box, no source).

As you plan your menus, look at your family calendar. Write down if you know you will be eating out, away from home, have an early soccer game, etc. I know that on nights that I tutor I will want to use a meal from the freezer or a crock-pot recipe. I try to save new recipes for nights when I won't be quite so rushed. Post the menu plan on the refrigerator door. In the morning I can get out the meat for my meal. My family often checks out the menu during the week.

I typically don't plan lunches. We have a fairly regular repertoire of things to have for lunch and I try to keep those ingredients on hand. Summer time is the exception. I do occasionally plan lunches in the summer around our summer "kids are home from school and life is crazy" schedules. Some of our favorite summer lunches include; tortilla roll-ups, pita sandwiches, quesadillas, fresh fruit kabobs, fish sticks, chicken nuggets and good old macaroni and cheese.

Master shopping lists have made grocery shopping much more enjoyable for me. Yes, I said "enjoyable." I get a quirky little thrill over completing my shopping without ever doubling back through aisles for missed items. I have also learned that I can complete my shopping for a two week menu plan in just under sixty minutes and that is with two toddlers in tow! It is not difficult to create a family shopping list on the computer, listing all the foods and other grocery store items your family consumes. It's especially nice if your grocery store has a store map available. Then you can modify your personal shopping list according to the order you shop the store. Print several copies and post them on the refrigerator. Help your family learn to mark the items that they use up so they can be replaced. I have already created a master shopping list for you. It is included at the end of this chapter. You can certainly make copies of this master list for yourself. However, if you don't have a copying machine in your home, and not many of us do, then it may be easier for you to use these lists as a pattern for creating your own lists on your personal computer. Doing this allows you to print a new list whenever necessary.

Be flexible. If a better offer comes up, the 2-year-old has the flu and you need to hold him all day, or you have a headache, bag the meal plan and shoot for the frozen pizza! A word of warning, if you will be postponing someone's favorite meal, be sure that you schedule it again soon. In fact, I like to schedule one night a month as "Cook's Choice." That's the night I slip in a previously missed meal or we do leftovers.

Save your menu planning sheets! I often look back at past menus and simply copy them. I also mark recipes that I tried that were new, and indicate whether or not they were a hit.

Tips on Grocery Shopping

- Use your menus to create your grocery list BEFORE you go to the store.

- ONLY buy what is on your list and what you need. At the end of the two weeks my fridge is very bare!

- Plan your menus around sales.

- Don't shop at only one store. However, don't shop at several stores. Choose two or three and stick with them.

- Avoid prepackaged and preprocessed high-priced items. You can save money if you shop primarily around the perimeter of the store where the fresh produce, meat, and dairy can be found.

- Modify your menus to include some meatless nights.

- Never buy bottle juices. You'll notice they all say "from concentrate." That means that you are paying for someone else's water! Always buy frozen.

- Never shop when you are hungry or tired.

- Shop with cash. You become a more attentive shopper when you know that you don't have a checkbook or credit card to come to your rescue at the cash register. This will make you stick to your list for sure!

- Coupon Alert! Coupons ONLY save you money if they are for items you would typically buy even without a coupon.

- Store brands are often cheaper than name brands with a coupon. I used to be a name brand snob when it came to buying groceries. Let's face it, some store brand items taste really nasty, but others are exactly the same as the more expensive name brand. Today there are only a few items that I really insist on the name brand, but for many things the store brand works just fine.

- Find out if your grocery store doubles coupons and which days.

- Shop less often. When you start planning menus for two weeks at a time and shop accordingly, you will waste less, use less, and save more.

- Drink water. Always offer water before juice or pop. If my family is still thirsty after they drink water, then they are welcome to have something more costly to drink.

- Go to your thrift bakery outlet. In Rochester, I go to Wonder Hostess Thrift Shop or Holsum-Taystee Bakery Outlet. These stores usually have fresh products at large discount prices. Note: always check dates on your products.

- Quit your job as a short-order chef. When you fix a meal for your family and one child refuses to eat it and wants PB and J and another now wants mac and cheese, the cost of the meal increases significantly. Stick to your meal plan and let your family know that this is what's being served until breakfast the next morning. One trick I learned from another "seasoned" mom is to make sure that I always have something on the table that I know they will eat (i.e. apple slices, cheese, bread and butter, etc.). Rarely has anyone had to leave the table hungry.

- Don't shop with your kids if you can help it.

- Shop at Sam's Club IF you watch prices. You CAN save money doing this, but you do need to be price savvy. Also, buying in bulk can save you money because it decreases the number of trips you make to the store. However, it will do you no good if you aren't aware of the shelf life of items and they end up spoiling before they are used. Use discretion.

- Load up on the loss leaders. Loss Leaders are the advertised items on the front of the sale flyer that the store used to lure you into the store. Now is the time to stock up on these items. We recently bought ten pizzas for $10 and ten cans of mushrooms for $2. Consequently, I can feed my whole family on one pizza topped with extra mushrooms for $1.20. That sure beats $17 at a pizza delivery place!

- Store cottage cheese and sour cream containers up-side down in the refrigerator. They will last twice as long.

- Keep an inventory of your pantry and freezer.

- Keep your freezer full. A full freezer runs more efficiently. If you can't keep it full of food, fill it with jugs of water.

- Freeze food in ziploc bags. Lay the bag filled with food on the counter and make it flat. Then squeeze out all of the air. I have even gone so far as to use a straw and suck out the extra air. Then freeze the food stacked up flat.

- Compare the cost-per-unit for items. This simply means dividing the cost of the packaged food item by the number of items or servings in the package.

- Cleaning products, over-the-counter drugs, and paper products are usually cheaper at discount stores than at the grocery store.

Still spending too much on food?

The following are 5 ways to save more money on food:

1. Eat at home more often. Save dining out as a treat, not a habit. Menu planning will really help eliminate excessive spending at restaurants.

2. Watch serving sizes. We Americans often think that bigger is better. Typically our servings are 2-3 times what they should be. Start to think smaller.

3. Avoid buying lots of snack foods like chips, cookies, candy, pop, etc.

4. Use leftovers or reduce recipe sizes. We rarely have leftovers because I look at the servings on recipes and only fix 5 servings for the 5 of us. I never thought I would be able to feed my family on 1 lb. of chicken, but that is exactly what I do now. Mixed with vegetables or pasta or rice, they don't seem to notice that there is less meat and they tend to clean it all up!

5. Watch expiration dates and foods that spoil quickly. This is another problem that seems to ease if you follow your menu plan.

Money Saving Substitutes:

When my time is in more abundance than my money, I have occasionally made some family favorites from scratch.

Chocolate Syrup (like Hershey's Syrup)

- *1 cup cocoa powder, unsweetened*
- *2 cups sugar*
- *1/4 teaspoon salt*
- *1 ¼ cup water*
- *1 tablespoon vanilla*

In a 1-qt. saucepan, combine the cocoa, sugar and salt. Mix together so that no cocoa lumps remain. Add the water and stir. Turn on heat to medium and stir occasionally until the sugar is dissolved (but do not boil), then remove from heat. Stir in the vanilla.

Store in a jar in the refrigerator for 2-3 months. It will become very thick when it is cold, but thins out once reheated (use low heat and constant stirring to reheat).

Casserole Sauce Mix

(Substitutes for a can of Cream Soup. I really like this!)

- 2 cups nonfat dry milk
- ¾ cup cornstarch
- ¼ cup instant chicken bouillon (or other flavor)
- 2 tablespoons dried minced onion flakes
- 1 teaspoon dried basil, crushed
- 1 teaspoon dried thyme
- ½ teaspoon pepper

Yield: 3 cups mix (equivalent to about 9 cans of soup)

Combine all ingredients, mixing well. Store in airtight container.

To use Casserole Sauce Mix: Combine 1/3-cup mix with 1-cup water in saucepan. Cook and stir until thickened. Or, to save pans, add mix and water to browned and drained casserole meat and cook in skillet with other casserole ingredients. Use instead of canned soup in any casserole.

This sauce is similar to purchased condensed soup. However, it has about 1/3 the calories and sodium and about 1/100th the fat. Canned soup adds 300 calories to your casserole – this adds 95. You may want to make up a couple of batches, with *different flavors of bouillon. Expect to save $7-$9 by making this from scratch instead of buying cans of Cream Soup.*

Homemade Stock or Broth

Save all vegetable peelings from carrots, onions and celery to make into the most delicious broth! Simply wash the vegetable before peeling and then peel your vegetable (for whatever recipe you are preparing). Keep a large container in your freezer into which you can continually add these vegetable peelings. When the container is full dump it into a large pan, cover it with water, bring it to a boil and then simmer for 1 -1 1/2 hours. Strain it and you have an absolutely FREE vegetable broth...don't pay $$$ for canned broth when you can have a more flavorful (the most intense flavor of the vegetable is in the peel) broth that is also more nutritious, quick and easy.

Chicken broth can be made just as easily by saving chicken bones in the freezer from when you either buy the meat on the bone and cut it off yourself or save a carcass from a roast chicken. Add the vegetable peelings and water, bring to a boil and then simmer for 1 1/2-hours. You can use many different vegetables; however, stay away from broccoli, cauliflower, cabbage and fresh herbs as they all give up a bitter taste if simmered over a long period of time.

Egg Substitute

- 2 large egg whites, lightly beaten
- 1 tablespoon nonfat dry milk powder
- 1 teaspoon vegetable oil
- 4 drops yellow food coloring

Yield: ¼ cup egg substitute = 1 large egg

Ketchup

- 1 quart tomato juice
- 1 onion, chopped
- 1 cup sugar
- ½ cup vinegar
- 1 teaspoon salt
- 1/3 red pepper
- 1 teaspoon celery salt

Mix. Boil for 30 minutes; then add 1 heaping tablespoon cornstarch mixed with a little water. Cook until it thickens. Can while hot in jars and seal. This has a one year shelf life if unopened and a 4-6 month shelf life if opened and stored in the refrigerator.

Forms that Follow:

Menu Planning

Freezer Inventory

Pantry Inventory

Master Grocery List for Hyvee-Barlow

Resources:

Barnes, Emilie. *More Hours In My Day*. Harvest House, 1982.

Cilley, Marla. *Sink Reflections*. Bantam, 2002.

Family Circle 2000 Hints and Tips, Doubleday, 2000.

Hunt, Mary. *The Complete Cheapskate*. Focus on the Family, 1997.

McCoy, Jonni. *Frugal Families*. Bethany House, 1998.

Savage, Jill. *Professionalizing Motherhood*. Zondervan, 2001.

Menu Plan

Month _____

Source:	Source:	Source:
Source:	Source:	Source:
Source:	Source:	Source:
Source:	Source:	Source:

Freezer Inventory

Date Inventory Taken _____

_____ ☐☐☐☐☐☐☐☐☐

_____ ☐☐☐☐☐☐☐☐☐

_____ ☐☐☐☐☐☐☐☐☐

_____ ☐☐☐☐☐☐☐☐☐

_____ ☐☐☐☐☐☐☐☐☐

_____ ☐☐☐☐☐☐☐☐☐

_____ ☐☐☐☐☐☐☐☐☐

_____ ☐☐☐☐☐☐☐☐☐

_____ ☐☐☐☐☐☐☐☐☐

_____ ☐☐☐☐☐☐☐☐☐

_____ ☐☐☐☐☐☐☐☐☐

_____ ☐☐☐☐☐☐☐☐☐

_____ ☐☐☐☐☐☐☐☐☐

Put a check mark in each box to record each item in your freezer.
Cross out each item if used or removed.
/ = item put in freezer   x = item used or out

Pantry Inventory
Date Inventory Taken _____

_____ ☐☐☐☐☐☐☐☐☐

_____ ☐☐☐☐☐☐☐☐☐

_____ ☐☐☐☐☐☐☐☐☐

_____ ☐☐☐☐☐☐☐☐☐

_____ ☐☐☐☐☐☐☐☐☐

_____ ☐☐☐☐☐☐☐☐☐

_____ ☐☐☐☐☐☐☐☐☐

_____ ☐☐☐☐☐☐☐☐☐

_____ ☐☐☐☐☐☐☐☐☐

_____ ☐☐☐☐☐☐☐☐☐

_____ ☐☐☐☐☐☐☐☐☐

_____ ☐☐☐☐☐☐☐☐☐

_____ ☐☐☐☐☐☐☐☐☐

Put a check mark in each box to record each item in your pantry.

Cross out each item if used or removed.

/ = item put in pantry   ✗ = item used or out

Master
Grocery List

Customer Service
- ☐ Film Developing
- ☐ Postage Stamps

Deli /Kitchen
- ☐ Fresh Meat
- ☐ Salads

Produce
- ☐ Broccoli
- ☐ Carrots
- ☐ Cauliflower
- ☐ Celery
- ☐ Cucumber
- ☐ Garlic
- ☐ Green Peppers
- ☐ Lettuce
- ☐ Mushrooms

Meat
- ☐ Ground Beef
- ☐ Steak
- ☐ Roast
- ☐ Pork Chops
- ☐ Pork Roast/ Ribs
- ☐ Chicken Breasts
- ☐ Turkey
- ☐ Sandwich Meat
- ☐ Hotdogs
- ☐ Fish Sticks
- ☐ Chicken Nuggets

Aisle 1
- ☐ Vitamins
- ☐ Tylenol
- ☐ Ibuprofen

- ☐ Feminine Pads
- ☐ Tampons

Aisle 2
- ☐ Juice
- ☐ Ketchup
- ☐ Mustard
- ☐ Pickles
- ☐ Jams/Jellies
- ☐ Peanut Butter
- ☐ Salad Dressings
- ☐ Mayonnaise
- ☐ Vinegar
- ☐ BBQ Sauce

Aisle 3
- ☐ Canned Peaches
- ☐ Canned Pears

- ☐ Spaghetti Sauce
- ☐ Pasta
- ☐ Egg Noodles
- ☐ Spaghetti Noodles

Aisle 4
- ☐ Gelatin/Pudding
- ☐ Cake Mix
- ☐ Cake Frosting
- ☐ Pie shells/Graham cracker crust
- ☐ Chocolate Chips
- ☐ Nuts
- ☐ Dried Fruit
- ☐ Cooking Oil
- ☐ Corn Syrup

- [ ] Onions
- [ ] Potatoes
- [ ] Tomato
- [ ] Apples
- [ ] Bananas
- [ ] Berries
- [ ] Grapes
- [ ] Oranges
- [ ] Peaches/Pears

Bakery

- [ ] Cakes
- [ ] Donuts
- [ ] Rolls

- [ ] Cough Medicine /Decongestant
- [ ] Bandages/Gauze
- [ ] Antibiotic Creme
- [ ] Toothpaste /brush
- [ ] Dental Floss
- [ ] Contact Cleaner
- [ ] Shampoo
- [ ] Hair Conditioner
- [ ] Hair Spray
- [ ] Detangle Spray
- [ ] Hand/Body Soap
- [ ] Razor Blades
- [ ] Shaving Cream
- [ ] Hand/Body Lotion
- [ ] Cotton Balls
- [ ] Cotton Swabs
- [ ] Deodorant

- [ ] Fruit Cocktail
- [ ] Mandarin Oranges
- [ ] Cranberry Sauce
- [ ] Pineapple
- [ ] Apple Sauce
- [ ] Pie Filling
- [ ] Sweet Potatoes
- [ ] Canned Green Beans
- [ ] Canned Peas
- [ ] Canned Corn
- [ ] Canned Mixed Veg.
- [ ] Canned Mushrooms
- [ ] Tomato Sauce
- [ ] Tomato Paste
- [ ] Stewed Tomatoes

- [ ] Flour
- [ ] Biscuit Mix
- [ ] Corn Meal
- [ ] Sugar, granulated
- [ ] Brown Sugar
- [ ] Sugar Substitutes
- [ ] Shortening
- [ ] Non-Stick Spray
- [ ] Cocoa/Baking Choc.
- [ ] Salt/Pepper
- [ ] Spices
- [ ] Baking soda/powder
- [ ] Corn Starch
- [ ] Yeast

Aisle 5

- [ ] Instant Potatoes
- [ ] Soups
- [ ] Cream of Mushroom
- [ ] Cream of Chicken
- [ ] Chicken/Beef Bouillon
- [ ] Stuffing
- [ ] Gravy
- [ ] Pasta Meals
- [ ] Rice/Beans
- [ ] Pizza Kit
- [ ] Chinese Noodles
- [ ] Soy Sauce
- [ ] Tortilla Shells
- [ ] Taco Mix
- [ ] Salsa
- [ ] Tang, Kool-Aid
- [ ] Chips
- [ ] Candy

Aisle 8

- [ ] Cookies
- [ ] Snack Crackers
- [ ] Rice Cakes
- [ ] Bread, White
- [ ] Bread, Whole Wheat
- [ ] Bagels
- [ ] English Muffins
- [ ] Buns
- [ ] Melba Toast
- [ ] Bread Sticks
- [ ] Office Supplies
- [ ] Batteries
- [ ] Film
- [ ] Auto/Hardware
- [ ] Bird Food
- [ ] Magazines

Aisle 11

- [ ] Household Cleaners
- [ ] Oven Cleaner
- [ ] Carpet Deodorizer
- [ ] Air Freshener
- [ ] Disinfectant
- [ ] Brooms/Mops
- [ ] Dishwasher Detergent
- [ ] Dish Soap
- [ ] Laundry Detergent
- [ ] Clothes Softener

Dairy

- [ ] Eggs
- [ ] Milk
- [ ] Coffee Creamer
- [ ] Egg Substitute
- [ ] Cheese, Cheddar
- [ ] Cheese, Mozzarella
- [ ] Cheese, Sliced
- [ ] Cheese, Processed
- [ ] Cheese, Parmesan
- [ ] Yogurt
- [ ] Butter/Margarine
- [ ] Sour Cream
- [ ] Cottage Cheese
- [ ] Cream Cheese
- [ ] Biscuits
- [ ] Pie Crusts

- ☐ Canned Beef/Chicken
- ☐ Tuna
- ☐ Chili

Aisle 6
- ☐ Cereal
- ☐ Granola Bars
- ☐ Fruit Snacks
- ☐ Oatmeal
- ☐ Pancake Mix
- ☐ Maple Syrup
- ☐ Toys
- ☐ Snack Cakes

Aisle 7
- ☐ Snacks
- ☐ Nuts
- ☐ Popcorn/Pretzels

Aisle 9
- ☐ Tea (bag/instant)
- ☐ Coffee
- ☐ Hot Cocoa Mix
- ☐ Chocolate Syrup
- ☐ Health Foods
- ☐ Low Sugar Foods

Aisle 10
- ☐ Diapers
- ☐ Baby Needs
- ☐ Baby Formula
- ☐ Baby Food
- ☐ Baby
- ☐ Soap/Lotion
- ☐ Dog Food
- ☐ Cat Food
- ☐ Pet Supplies
- ☐ Cat Litter

- ☐ Bleach/Stain Remover

Aisle 12
- ☐ Light Bulbs
- ☐ Toilet Paper
- ☐ Cups/Plates
- ☐ Facial Tissues
- ☐ Charcoal
- ☐ Aluminum Foil
- ☐ Waxed Paper
- ☐ Plastic Wrap
- ☐ Storage Bags
- ☐ Paper Towels
- ☐ Garbage Bags
- ☐ Napkins

Aisle 13
- ☐ Pop
- ☐ Water

- ☐ Refrigerated Juices

Frozen
- ☐ Orange Juice
- ☐ Waffles
- ☐ French Toast
- ☐ Dinners
- ☐ Broccoli
- ☐ Mixed Veg.
- ☐ Whole Corn
- ☐ Green Beans
- ☐ Pizza
- ☐ Ice Cream
- ☐ French Fries
- ☐ Tater Tots
- ☐ Whipped Toppings
- ☐ Fruit
- ☐ Desserts

NOTES

Saving Money in

Rochester

*"Rejoice in all the good things
the Lord your God has given
to you and your household."
Deuteronomy 26:11*

How fortunate we are to live in a city that is growing in
population but hasn't lost the "small town" feeling. Rochester
provides many free or inexpensive activities to experience with
your spouse and children. Some of the following ideas are just

the beginning to incorporate learning, quality time, and feeding and clothing your family with minimal expense.

Allie Pleiter, the author of Becoming a Chief Home Officer, tells of how she had to rethink how she spent money when she became a stay-at-home mom. She didn't realize that discount stores did offer fashions at lower prices because she had never shopped there prior to this time in her life. Yes, I have friends who claim that their clothes from Anne Klein are of better quality, and I don't doubt that. But, I would be horrified to have food stains from sticky fingers on a blouse that cost $80! The way to shop is to buy classic pieces that will not go out of style and buy new pieces as you sell or donate old pieces. My pastor's wife takes advantage of the sweater sales at Kohl's each year. She buys one or two new sweaters to replace old ones. This system works for her so she isn't buying an entire wardrobe at one time. Spend the time looking at clothing ads in the paper and comparison shop. Some stores offer the same brand, but at different prices. Ask if a store will price match another store's ads. Wal-Mart is very good about this if you bring in the ad from the other store. Go on the store's web site and look for store coupons if you don't have access to their flyers in the paper. Remember: keep a list of your family's current clothing and shoe sizes with you. This way you may be shopping for something like table linens and see the children's department is having a great sale. I take advantage of end-of-season sales and buy for the next year. Carter's pajamas sell for approximately $15 - $22 per pair. I wait until Kohl's has a sale and get them for approximately $8 a pair. I buy brand name on pajamas because of the frequency of wear and for warmth or breathable materials that are also fire retardant.

Another way to save money is to know what you already have in the closet and drawers. In the beginning, I would purchase items I already owned, but couldn't find or see. This cost me money to have duplicates. I routinely go through my closets and drawers and thin them out by taking some to consignment, donate, or toss if they are stained and have holes. I label Rubbermaid type storage tubs with sizes and contents on the lids. I am in the process of doing this for my sweaters since I like to purchase a couple new ones each season and get rid of worn ones. Sometimes I have purchased the exact one I am tossing because I didn't realize I had one just like it!

Clothing

Retail stores mark up the price of clothing so they can make a profit. A former co-worker of mine worked in retail and gave me this little tip. When you go to a store for a sale, the clothing is still marked so the merchant is making a good margin in profits. When it is marked down to 75% -90% off, it is close to the actual price the merchant paid for the clothing! Paying even 50% off may be too much for what you get. There are several ways to have quality clothing without paying a lot for them.

*Exchange clothing-I did this for my son Drew. He received hand-me downs, and we gave clothing he hadn't grown into in exchange. When each child no longer could use the clothing, we returned it to each other to use for another child or to sell. This worked from birth to age three years.

I have also exchanged women's clothing with others. Have a "clothing swaps party" where you go through your closets and remove items you no longer can wear or haven't worn in a year. Set a night to invite others over to bring their clothes, too. Have each person select two articles of clothing. This is a great way to get new-to-you clothing without paying and also cleaning out your closet at the same time.

Garage sales-Each Wednesday in the free Rochester Business Guide delivered to your home and Wednesday through Friday in the Rochester Post Bulletin garage sales are listed by area of town. Also provided is a handy map to help you in your search. This works great, but be prepared for crowds and thoroughly look over clothing before buying.

I have purchased the next season clothing, clothing for the next year, shoes, and boots this way. It is becoming more difficult as Drew is getting older to find gently used clothing in his sizes. I also shop for sweatshirts for myself and husband to wear when we are doing chores and yard work.

Living in a city the size of Rochester makes it easy to get from one sale to the next. Use your map and read through all the garage sale ads a day or night before to "map" out your strategy. After doing this several times, you will be able to discern which sales will be better to meet your needs.

My personal advice: arrive 15 minutes early before the first sale begins. Don't expect to shop at that time, but there will be others lined up ready to shop as soon as they can. The competition is fierce for children's clothing. Expect it to be like the Christmas sales in the mall!

Consignment stores

In the past few years, Rochester has opened several consignment clothing stores in convenient locations. Consignment stores offer quality, newer and used clothing for a reasonable price. Some specialize in infants/children, women, or children/adult clothing. The first four stores listed are stores we have personally shopped and sold items.

Refashion Consigned Furniture and Clothing - 281-0808,

321 S. Broadway

The store is nicely laid out to make shopping easier. You will find name-brand clothing for a fraction of the original price. A former co-worker had found a certain line of clothing there, and we couldn't tell it was used!

All in VOGUE Collections - 286-8811

Miracle Mile Shopping Center,

126 17th Avenue

This store has clothing for all ages and sizes. Only accepts clothing three years old or less.

Children's Exchange - 289-6637

1249 Marion Rd.

Many items to choose. Both new and used clothing items, toys, books, and infant equipment. I have sold clothes there and received a fair price. Attached in a separate location is a maternity exchange as well.

Once Upon a Child - 252-5090

1115 Civic Center Drive NW (Barlow Plaza). New and used children's clothing, toys, and toddler/infant equipment.

Thrift Stores

Rochester has three major thrift stores in convenient locations. All stores carry clothing, books, music, videos, household items, and some toys. You may want to call and find out when they have special sales.

Community Clothesline Inc. - 282-8050

814 11th Avenue NE, Rochester. This is a smaller store that is located near Silver Lake Park. Clothing for children and adults, books, house wares, toys, games used and new.

Goodwill Industries Inc. - 281-9651

660 37th Street NW, Rochester.

Next to Hy-Vee Foods North

The surprise I found in this store was that it does carry items that are new from Target. They are marked as new and at reduced prices. The store is clean, fairly well spaced apart racks, and the staff is pleasant. Items do get tossed around from all the shoppers, so you do need to spend some time sorting through bins of shoes and bags. I have bought new shoes from there for $1! You may want to call and ask when special sales will be held.

The Salvation Army Thrift Store - 281-1561

115 1st Ave. NE, Rochester

This store carries clothing for all ages. When I visited there, it appeared they carried less clothing and more household items. If you have the time, shop there frequently because the inventory changes daily.

Super Shopping Centers

Over the last three years, Rochester has experienced the growth of Wal-Mart and Target into Super Centers. Along with K-Mart,

SAM'S and ShopKo, there are more options in choosing inexpensive clothing.

K-Mart - 288-9567

201 Ninth St SE

I personally have bought maternity clothing, children's clothing and women's wear at Rochester K-Mart and it has withstood wear. I like the Sesame Street brand children's clothing and have been fortunate enough to take advantage of a child's shoe sale-buy one, get second at half-price.

SAM'S Club - 281-8355

3410 55th Street NW

SAM'S offers clothing for adults and children, including name brands. I am pleased with the quality. The downside: there are no dressing rooms to try on clothing. The upside is that you can do one-stop shopping here!

ShopKo - 281-0656

3708 Hwy. 63 North

-or-

281-0686

2820 Hwy. 63 South

I like to shop at ShopKo because it is smaller, the staff is more personable, and the lines are shorter. I fill prescriptions there. The store-brand children's clothing tends to wear out quickly. When the clothing is around $3 for shirts or pants, I do buy some for play. The adult clothing varies in price and quality. ShopKo sells Nike brand and Payless Shoes. ShopKo also carries milk and non-perishable food items.

Target Super Store - 536-2555

3827 Market Place Drive NW

I find top designer names on everything from baby items to adult clothing and shoes. Consumer's Report Magazine stated the Cherokee brand polo shirts wear better than Polo brand. I like the toddler boy's sweat shirts and pants. They wear better than Garanimal's brand at Wal-Mart. Target can have some good sales and clearance rack items toward the end of the season. Starbuck's Coffee shop and the Pizza Hut are located in the snack shop.

Wal-Mart Super Centers - 280-7733   3400 NW 55th Street

-or-

292-0909 25 25th Street SE.

Wal-Mart offers everything at low prices. I love the Wal-Mart diapers called White Cloud. They cost less and worked just as well. I also liked the regular onesies or shirts and shorts. When Drew was young and not as active, they wore well. Wal-Mart will match prices if you bring the ad from another store.

Other shopping sources:

Apache Mall - Highway 52 South and 14 East, Rochester, MN. Apache Mall has four anchor stores: JC Penney, Sears, Herberger's and Marshall Fields. Each stock their own labels as well as name-brand labels. I have bought adult and children's clothing at each. Marshall Fields has great pre-and post-season sales and a good 13-hour sales. JC Penney and Herberger's have frequent sales, just ask when the next one will be. Sears has great sales in the children's department. Also, we belong to a frequent buying program for children's clothing. Each time we buy an item, we earn money. The buying program is free to join and the information is kept in the computer so no card to carry! Children's Place, The Disney Store, Gap Kids, and Gymboree all offer a variety of styles and prices. Ask for sale dates. Sign up to be on the store's mailing list. Also, note: Gap usually marks down clothing on Wednesday and when the price ends in $ .97, example, $4.97, this is a clue that it is at the final mark down price, so snatch it up! Avoid in-store credit card or reward points since they are designed to get the consumer to spend more for a small reward of $10-$25 coupons periodically.

TJ Maxx - 288-8966   1300 Salem Rd. SW

This store is home to adult and children's clothing at a reduced price. Names such as Anne Klein can be found there, as well as Tommy Hilfiger, Sag Harbor, and others. Please look over clothing carefully for snags, missing buttons and stains.

Medford Outlet Center - Interstate N 35 Medford, MN

(Near Owatonna)

Check out their website at **www.medfordoutlet.com**. Outlet centers offer a variety of brand name clothing styles. Be careful! Some stores cost as much as retail and offer lower quality clothing. Good times to shop are during holidays, before school, after Christmas, and Spring, when the next season of clothing is being advertised. If you go to the Mall Office or Dress Barn and ask for a FREE coupon packet, you can enjoy additional savings with coupons for many of the outlet stores.

Movie Savings

Movie Rentals-

Blockbuster Movies - 455 11th Avenue NW and 2800 41st St. NW.
Checkout Blockbuster Rewards, a program that costs you $10
to join. In return you get deals on buy one, get one free, coupons
periodically for a free movie rental, etc. The Rewards program is
for one year, and they do let you know when it will be expiring, so
there isn't a hidden, automatic renewal.

Hollywood Video - located on the corner of 37th Street NW and
West River Parkway NW. They have in store promotions as well
as five- day rentals on all new releases.

Premiere Video - near the Crossroads Shopping Center and
across from the Fairgrounds SE. They have an in store special
called "Hot Shot" which features a new release for a month at
the low price of $.99!

Hy-Vee Grocery Stores - all locations have a small movie rental
section that can be very handy to pick up a movie while shopping.

How about renting a movie and sharing it between two families?
Invite another family over for a fun "movie night" and they bring

the popcorn and munchies, or split the cost of the rental and watch it then give to the next family and they return it after they have watched it. Also the Public Library and Book Mobile have videos and DVD's available for adults and children.

Movie Theatres -

Chateau Theatres - 536-4769

Next to Shopko on East Circle Drive NE Discount tickets available to ALL area businesses for employee use. Movies (matinee) up to 6pm are $5 Evening prices for adults $7; Seniors & children under 12 years $5

Please visit our website at **www.chateautheatres.com** for complete information about: eTicketing, Food Court, Kids Shows, Senior Movie, Reel Babies, Encore Classics, Live Music and so much more...

Cinemagic Stadium 12 - 280-0333

West Circle Drive and 19th street NW They accept discount tickets. Matinee movies and all movies up to 6pm are $5; evening prices for adults: $7, Seniors 60 and over, children 11 years and under: $5. Go to **ww.rochestermn.com** for all the movie listings for the week.

Kid-Friendly Restaurants

Eating out in the restaurant of our choice before children was a major part of our social lives. We would meet friends and have a nice, leisurely meal without interruptions. Remember those days? Well after my first child was born, we would still try to eat out, but not at some of the more intimate, couples' places. You know the ones: they don't have a kid's menu or highchairs. When our child became more vocal and squirmy, we resorted to eating out at fast-food types either dining in or driving through. I'm sharing this with you so you don't have to learn some of the lessons we did the hard way.

Just the other day we invited my husband to eat with us at Applebees over the noon hour. We have eaten there many times before but usually earlier or later in the day. Drew is familiar with Applebees and they try to be accommodating to his age group by providing crayons and color books, kid-sized-covered drink cups, and balloons. He was doing well for the first 10 minutes, but then decided that bouncing on the booth seat was much better. He was the only toddler there during a lunch hour and was a big distraction to many business lunches taking place. I learned not to expect others to be as charmed by my son as I am and to try and avoid "business crowds" if possible.

Good times to go with kids are generally:

11 - 11:30 a.m. Monday - Sunday,

5 p.m. Monday -Thursday

4:30 p.m. Friday – Saturday

5 p.m. on Sunday.

The following are restaurants we have found to be kid-friendly.

They are in alphabetical order.

*Leo's Pizza Palace – 2280 Superior Drive, NW

424-3711

Pizza, Breadsticks, and Salad, Games, Climbing Gym, Token

Redemption, and Leo the Lion visits with kids every hour, Target

Audience is toddler – 12   ***New as of 12/04**

Applebees Neighborhood Grill & Bar - 320 Apache Mall

252-0155

- or –

3794 Marketplace Dr. NW

280-6626

Kid menus, color crayons, coloring books, balloons, tables and

booths

Bon's Buffet - 1652 Hwy. 52 N

281-9699

Asian and American choices, booths and tables, busy lunch hour during the week

Bruegger's Bagels Bakeries -1201 S Broadway

287-0203

Variety of bagel flavors, juices, milk, tables and couches

Burger King Restaurants - 1021 15th Avenue SE - 282-4239

4107 Hwy. 52 N & Frontage Rd. -

281-2923

1550 N Broadway - 280-9357

615 S Broadway - 288-8932

2630 S Broadway - 536-9294

Tables and booths, fast food menu

Canadian Honker Restaurant & Catering - 1201 2nd Street SW

282-6572

Tables, busy lunch hour, American food

Carlos O'Kelly's - 4825 Hwy. 52 N

282-2590

Tables and booths, kid menu, possible long wait during a supper
hour on weekends, Mexican and American food

Chateau Movie Theatres - 3450 E Circle Dr. NE

536-7469

Large menu selection, eating area, opens at 11 a.m.

China Dynasty - 701 S Broadway - 289-2333

Tables and booths, friendly staff, busy lunch hour, known for the
large goldfish in a tank

The Coffee Mouse Café - 16th Street NW (Miracle Mile)

282-7711

Cozy environment, tables, friendly staff, sandwiches, soups,
desserts, beverages

Culver's — 3390 55th Street NW - 281-8538

- or -

36 28th Street St. SE - 282-3300

"Butter Burger", custard, fast food made to order, tables,
booths, and kids menu.

Dos Amigos Mexican Restaurants - 1611 Hwy. 52 N

536-4527

- or -

204th Street SE (seasonal outdoor seating)

282-3300

Tables and booths, kid menu, lively atmosphere, quick service, friendly wait staff

Fiesta Mexicana - 1645 N Broadway

(Northbrook Shopping Center)

288-1116.

Tables and booths, kid menu, lively atmosphere

Godfather's Pizza -1611 16th Street NW

(Hillcrest Shopping Center)

288-7515

Tables and booths, video games, family type atmosphere

Golden Corral - 2755 43rd Street NW

282-2180.

Children three and under eat free; children ages 4-12 eat for $1.99. Mondays are especially geared toward the "younger" crowd by providing a menu that caters to their taste, Mr. Magic to entertain the family.

Great China - 4214 Hwy. 52 N

280-9092

Tables and booths, seated quickly

Hanger Bar & Grill — 7386 Airport View Drive SE

288-1438

Sunday morning buffet, tables, kids eat free on Monday evenings

McDonalds Restaurants - 1306 Apache Drive SW (Playland)-

288-2264

1116 N. Broadway - 288-4454

1937 Frontage Rd. W - 252-0691

5500 Hwy. 52 N - 289-5289

Tables and booths, fast food menu

Mr. Pizza - 1729 S Broadway

288-1488

Good lunch specials, eat-in, carry-out, booths and tables

The Old Country Buffet - 1300 Salem Rd. SW

(TJ Maxx Shopping Center)

289-4617

Thursdays are family nights with the O.C. Bee character visiting tables handing out coloring sheets and balloons from 5p.m. to 8p.m.

Olive Garden Italian Restaurant - 380 17th Avenue NW

288-8722.

Tables and booths, kid menu; avoid 6 p.m. on Friday or Saturday evenings

The Outback Steakhouse - 120 S Broadway

252-1150

The restaurant now has call ahead option for seating; toys provided in the lobby, coloring books, crayons, table sized toys, and animal crackers

Panera Bread - 460 Crossroads Dr. SW

285-5800

- or –

3780 Marketplace Dr. NW

280-9185

Tables and booths, variety of bagel and pastry flavors, drinks, very busy place in the early morning and lunch time

Pizza Hut - Delivery or Carryout-840 S Broadway - **285-5000**

1105 7th Street NW - **252-1212**

Dine-in or Carryout-2001 Hwy. 52 - **287-6396**

Kid menus, color crayons, kid place mats, bibs, tables and booths

Pizza Man - 14 17th Avenue NW (Miracle Mile Shopping Center)

287-8700

Eat-in or take-out, good lunch specials, booths or tables

Red Lobster Restaurant - 195 S Broadway (Galleria Mall)

287-9710

Tables and booths, busy lunch hour, staff is accommodating to small children but tables are close together so if children are upset it may bother other patrons

Sky Dragon Buffet - 115 16th Avenue NW (Miracle Mile)

281-1813

Asian and limited American choices on buffet, tables and booths, busy lunch hour

TGIFriday's - 300 Hwy. 52 N

281-2020.

Tables and booths, American food, kid menu, crayons, Etch-a-Sketches

Valentino's Pizza & Pasta -130 Elton Hills Drive NW

281-2100

Tables only

Some tips on how to make dining out more cost-effective:

- Order water to drink.

- Share an entree with your mate.

- Skip the kids meals; order one entree or from ala carte menu and split between the kids.

- Order from the kids or appetizer menu for yourself; smaller portions help the diet!

- Go to eat during lunch or early bird hours.

- Use "two for one" coupons listed in the free Shopper newspaper or ads.

- Skip dessert, marked up prices for beverages, and dessert items.

- Order one entree and ask for a take home box right away; place half of the meal into the box and when you get home, immediately put in a freezer bag or container for a meal later.

- Check if restaurants offer a free beverage or dessert for your birthday.

- Go to buffet style restaurants for lunch; the same buffet will go up in price for supper.

Allie Pleiter, author of Becoming A Chief Home Officer, states that eating at her local grocery store with her two children each week before grocery shopping became an educational and special outing. She budgeted for this meal time, and it became a memorable experience for all. Her daughter tried different ethnic foods resulting in discussions about the people who lived in different parts of the world.

Some local places to try are:

Hy-Vee Grocery Stores - 500 37th Street NW - **289-0266**

500 Crossroads Drive SW - **289-7500**

1315 6th Street NW (Barlow Plaza) -

288-8233

Grill area and deli, open for breakfast. Hy-Vee South has a food island where you can try Asian and Italian foods.

SAM'S Club - 3410 55th Street NW

281-8355

Small grill, pizza, snack foods and dining area

Target - 3827 Marketplace Dr. NW

536-2555

Small grill & snack foods, Pizza Hut, dining area

Wal-Mart Supercenter - 3400 55th Street NW

280-7733

- or -

25 25th Street SE - **292-0909**

Pizza by pie or slice, hot dogs, snack foods, and dining area

Resource:

Pleiter, Allie. *Becoming a Chief Home Officer.* Zondervan, 2002.

Inexpensive Dates

"Therefore encourage one another

and

Build each other up."

1Thesselonians 5:11 NIV

☺   Plan a date on a teen's budget. Try a local burger establishment and share a malt. Go see a movie and sit in the back row for a little handholding.

☺   Why not try a game of miniature golf or head to a putting green? If the weather doesn't cooperate, then head indoors to the bowling alley. Play for a pizza or beverages.

☺   Rent a canoe or paddleboat (Silver Lake) and go to the center of the lake. Read romantic poems or make up your own.

☺   Pick your favorite public bench and invite your honey to a bench brunch date complete with bagels, cream cheese, and coffee.

☺ Spend time together while helping others. Nonprofit organizations often put out a call for volunteers around major holidays. Some local needs: Channel One Food Shelf, Dorothy Day House, Christmas Anonymous, and the Salvation Army to name a few.

☺ Make a cozy homemade Italian dinner. Set the mood with an Italian opera playing in the background (look at the library for selections).

Dig in Your Pocket Dates

$ Plan to stay overnight either near by or a couple of hours away at a bed and breakfast. Be tourists and check out museums, shops, and recreation. A fun place to go, even for adults, is Wisconsin Dells!

$ Steal away to the Chanhassen Dinner Theatre for good food and musical entertainment.

$ Choose a nice, local restaurant and ask for a cozy table for two. Afterwards take an evening stroll and wish upon a star.

$ Find a common interest, such as theatre, sporting events, or music and invest in season tickets. To lessen the expense, invite a couple to share the cost and divide the tickets.

$ Make the time to learn a new skill together. Never skied? Rent skis and take lessons together. Sign up for ballroom dance lessons. Peruse the Community Education brochure for ideas.

Creative Cost Conscious Babysitting Solutions

Exchange babysitting time with another family with similar values and parenting style. Create a schedule for each month so each couple has a chance to go out on a date and also takes a turn sitting for the other family.

In exchange for babysitting time, provide a free service for a family, high-school, or college-aged students. For example, provide a meal, yard work, or run errands for a busy family. Or, provide tutoring or transportation services for students.

A babysitting cooperative is also a good idea. To create a cooperative consider the following steps:

- determine the number of families involved-five is a good number

- establish a token system, for example, each family receives a set amount of poker chips to "cash in" for sitting services; each poker chip is worth one hour of babysitting time per child

- each family has the option of declining sitting services if it doesn't work in their schedule

- each time a family does provide sitting services, they get to keep the poker chips, thus earning them more sitting time

- once a family is out of poker chips, they can earn more by offering sitting services

- determine certain days and times that work for each family to sit

- create a list of names, ages of children, addresses, and phone numbers of the families participating

- if a family declines to sit and doesn't "cash in" tokens for services within four-six months, find out if they still want to participate in the cooperative-if not, find another family to join

- every six months evaluate how the cooperative is working and make changes

Let's Get Organized

"She watches over the affairs of her household

and does not eat the bread of idleness"

Proverbs 31:27

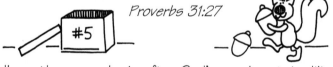

A Godly mother, one who is after God's own heart, is diligent in
her home. Proverbs 31:27 reminds us that this is God's
instruction for us as mothers and wives. As I consider
everything involved in "watching over the affairs of (my)
household," I am struck by the fact that this is a tremendous
responsibility that I am called to do! When I am managing the
affairs of my home I am creating a place where my family's
hearts don't have to be troubled. The world that we live in can be

pretty chaotic, but the orderly home that I create for my family can be their haven. With that in mind, in this chapter we hope to give you a sampling of some of the tricks and techniques that have helped us create order and organization in our homes.

Keep a Master Calendar

I suggest a large calendar that shows the entire month on one page and has large squares for each day. We keep ours on the refrigerator. Office supply stores carry these. Ours has a white board to the right of the calendar, which is also handy.

This calendar is the control center of your family. As soon as the kids bring home papers from school, transfer dates to the calendar and dispose of the paper to avoid the "Paper Clutter Trap." The same thing can be done for church events, soccer, mother's groups etc. Birthdays and anniversaries can also be tracked on the calendar. I try to color code events if possible. Assign each family member a color and write their activities in that color.

The master calendar is also a nice place to jot down accomplishments of the kids that you can later transfer to their scrapbooks or baby books.

To Do Lists

In the morning or before you go to bed, make a "to-do" list. See the "Call-Do-See" list, suggested by Emilie Barnes, with the forms at the end of this chapter. On this form you:

1. List people you need to **call** and their phone numbers.

2. Jot down tasks you need to **do** (i.e. take clothes to dry cleaners, return books to library).

3. Note jobs you need to **see** completed (i.e. That Kadi practices piano, Ben's swimming lesson at 1:30 p.m., meet husband for lunch at noon, Watch American Idol on TV at 7:30 p.m.).

"To Do" lists are the best way to avoid procrastination. Some days there are so many things that need to be accomplished that it is easy to become overwhelmed and because you don't know where to begin, you never do begin.

As you tackle your list, do the things you like the least FIRST! Doing this will eliminate the dread that you feel until it is done. Once the nasty jobs are done you will have a better attitude about accomplishing the rest of your "To Do" list. For example, I personally clean my bathrooms and scrub my kitchen floor first when I clean my house. The rest of the house gets cleaned much faster after those jobs are done!

Speaking of Procrastination

The second part of Proverbs 31:27 reminds us that this excellent woman "...does not eat the bread of idleness." As this proverb suggests, we have a responsibility to eliminate idleness from our lives. Be aware of some of these things which may be robbing you of precious time:

- Inadequate personal planning. The reason things may not go according to plan is that you never had a plan.

- Too much phone time. Use a timer to make yourself more aware of the time you do spend and don't hesitate to tell people that it's not a good time for you to talk. Don't accept phone solicitations. Let the answering machine pick up messages during meal times. Call people when you

know they won't be home and leave them a short
message, if you don't have time to talk.

- Telemarketing calls. Have your phone number taken off telemarketing lists. See the Family Resource Chapter for addresses and phone numbers. It takes only seconds and you will see a noticeable decrease in the number of telemarketing calls you receive.

- Surfing the Web. If you absolutely MUST get on the Internet, get your other work done first and then set a timer to keep yourself honest.

- Learn to delegate. See the section on chores later in this chapter.

- Don't read junk mail. In fact, set your recycling bin next to you while you go through the mail and pitch it! The same is true for reading lots of advertisements. Unless you are shopping for something specific, reading ads only makes you want things you may not be able to afford or may not really need.

- Keep a close check on your TV time. Turn the TV off at mealtime and try to have a couple of "no-TV" nights each week. Make it a story night, game night, or do family devotions with your kids!

Tickler File: A system to tickle your memory

This system was adopted from Emilie Barnes and modified by adding ideas from "The FlyLady" and me.

Purchase 3x5 cards and a box, ten in each of these colors: blue, yellow, pink, white, green, orange, and cherry, tabbed section dividers, or just buy a spiral bound notecard system with colored cards.

Section 1: Things you do DAILY. List all those things that you have to do daily in your house in order to maintain it. I sort mine by time of day. It says:

> Morning; Pray and read bible, Make beds, Pick-up the house, Do the dishes, Check the bathrooms, Thaw supper (meat), and Start laundry.
>
> Afternoon; Sort mail, Fix supper, Put the laundry away, Help with homework, Supervise piano practice.

Evening; Supper, Baths, Dishes, Pick-up house, Empty
dishwasher, Check AWANA memory verses, Read with
kids

Section 2: Things you do WEEKLY. You will have one card for
each day of the week. Mine looks like this:

Monday: Tutor, Sweep floors, Plan 2 week menus, Make
grocery list, Write Thank You notes and Greeting
cards (Keep these with your "Quiet" Time things.)

Tuesday; Mothers of Preschoolers (MOPS), Do grocery
shopping, Pay bills

Wednesday; Tutor, Water plants, Clean out fridge

Thursday; Clean house, Church fellowship group, Piano
lesson

Friday; Discipleship Group meets, "Catch-up day,"
Errands, Change bedding

Saturday and Sunday; Open

If you don't get to something on the list, don't do it the next
day. Rotate the cards and do it next week!

Section 3: Things you do MONTHLY. You will need to have
one card for each week of the month. For example:

Week 1: Clean out the car, Clean/organize the
coat/shoe closet, File bills

Week 2: Organize desk, Wash all rugs, Wash
decorator towels in the bathrooms

Week 3: Clean the oven, Do seasonal decorating,
Wash trashcans if needed

Week 4: Wash patio doors and front windows,
Clean ceiling fans

Section 4: Things you do QUARTERLY, SEMI-ANNUALLY, and
ANNUALLY. You will need one card for each month. This is
where you list things like: Check smoke detectors, Wash walls,
Clean the pantry, Wash curtains, De-Junk the house
(Described later in the chapter.), Wash windows, Straighten
drawers, Clean carpets

Section 5: This is where you record what is in your storage
boxes. See the section on De-Junking Your House

The "Tickler" file is meant to help you, not stress you out! You
can make it as detailed or as simple as you would like. If
something doesn't get done, "Let it go!" In the beginning, I was a
bit of a slave to my tickler file. After a couple of months it

became habit and I no longer referred to it as often. The key to the success of this organizational tool is that you do what works for you.

Laundry

This is where true confessions come in to play, because I am still working on this one! This is what the experts say and what I aspire to be able to do. If it counts in my favor, I believe that I can do this and you can too.

- There are 5 steps to doing laundry: sort, wash, dry, fold, put-away.

- Don't put in a load of laundry unless you finish it all the way through.

- Buy color-coded laundry baskets or make color-coded laundry bags for sorting. This can become a fun game for your kids, even the little ones! I would suggest white, dark, light, and bright.

- Replace all of your free wire hangers from the dry cleaners with plastic hangers. They are VERY cheep at dollar stores and discount stores. I recently bought packages of 13 hangers for $.88! Wire hangers are messy and they crease your clothing.

Save money with these great homemade cleaning products:

Laundry Softener

- *2 cups white vinegar*
- *2 cups baking soda*
- *4 cups water*

Combine slowly over a sink, because it will fizz. Pour into a plastic bottle, cover, and shake. Use ¼ cup in the final rinse or in a "Downy Ball."

Stain Remover

- *½ cup ammonia*
- *½ cup white vinegar*
- *2 Tablespoons liquid laundry detergent*
- *2 quarts water*

Mix well and store in a spray bottle.

Chores for Kids

Our pastor recently shared with the congregation that his wife had a unique interpretation of Proverbs 31:15, "...she provides food for her family and portions for her servant girls." Her interpretation was, "...she provides food for her family and "chores for her kids."

Children need to know that they are valuable and necessary members of the family and that their family doesn't operate well without their support. As mothers, we need to train our children, appreciate their accomplishments, and celebrate their capabilities. I am often guilty of not realizing my children's full potential to contribute to the family when I jump in and do everything that needs to be done.

Delegating responsibility to children is an important part of mothering. The following list is a compilation of suggestions from Emilie Barnes in More Hours in My Day and What Every Child Should Know Along the Way by Gail Martin. Please keep in mind that all children develop and mature differently. Some children will be doing these things earlier than listed and others will need more help and direction for longer before they master some of these tasks. When children are very young, do the chores with them. Assign chores that can be done successfully. Never debate whether or not a chore gets done, it just does! The Mother's Almanac says that, "No matter how you live, you have to do some routine housework every day and so should your child." If it helps, assign your children to odd or even days according to their birthdates. For example, Kadi's birthday in on the 13th and Caleb's is on the 22nd. So Kadi would do a particular chore on the odd days of the month and Caleb would do that chore on the even days. Finally, remember that "monkey see, monkey do." If you do your own chores and provide a model for your children, they will be more likely to do their chores as well.

The following are possible chores your children might be able to do.

Age 1:

     Help put away toys

Age 2:

     Undress self

     Put pajamas away

     Wash face and hands

     Pick up toys

     Clear off own place at table

Age 3:

Dress self

Make bed

Wipe up spills

Help set the table

Help clear the table

Put dirty clothes in the hamper (or in the color-coded bags/baskets)

Pick up toys

Brush hair with help

Brush teeth with help

Age 4:

Collect laundry

Pick up outside toys

Shake out area rugs

Dust and clean TV screen

Know own phone number (*We taught this earlier to the tune of BINGO, "At _____'s house there is a phone and this is _____'s number: _ _ _-_ _ _ _, _ _ _-_ _ _ _, _ _ _-_ _ _ _ (repeat entire phone number three times) and this is _____'s number!")

Know own address

Help empty dishwasher

Help bring in groceries

Know how to make emergency phone call (911)

Age 5:

Set the table

Clean the bathroom sink

Help clean and straighten drawers and closets

Clean up after pets

Feed pet

Walk the dog

Dust the furniture

Age 6:

Organize own drawers and closets

Empty dishwasher and put dishes away

Wash and dry dishes by hand

Straighten living and family rooms

Rake leaves

Clean mirrors

Bathe alone

Age 7:

Empty garbage

Help in kitchen after dinner

Help make lunch for school

Clean out car

Take piano lessons, etc.

Vacuum

Use a broom and dustpan

Take a written phone message

Read and prepare a simple recipe

Strip bed sheets

As your children grow and mature you can add more responsibilities such as:

Wash the car

Mow the lawn

Make meals and dessert

Clean refrigerator

Iron

Do yard work

The bottom line regarding chores and children is that the outcome of the job is not nearly as important as helping your children develop skills and capabilities and to encourage their efforts and contributions.

Paperwork

A simple organizational rule to remember is, "Don't put it down, put it away." This principle can be taken a step further when it comes to paperwork. Make every effort to handle a piece of mail only one time. Sort your mail over the trashcan as soon as you bring it into the house. Then sort what needs to be kept into three piles. You may choose to put them into three different colored file folders. I prefer to put mine into three stacking trays that sit on my desk. These folders/trays are marked, "TO READ," "TO PAY," or "TODAY." Only open the mail in the "TODAY" pile and deal with it immediately. Grab the "TO PAY" stuff on the day you are scheduled to pay bills (see your tickler file). When you know you will have to sit and wait somewhere (doctor's office, soccer or piano practice, etc.) take the "TO READ" pile with you.

When you have things organized you have more time to enjoy your family. Sometimes an annoyance can seem like a huge deal and can rob you of the joy of being with your family. Finding a phone number, remembering to whom you loaned your ladder, choosing the right size jeans for your husband, knowing your son's social security number for a form, or reporting a lost credit card are good examples. It makes you crabby and as the saying goes, "When Mamma ain't happy, ain't nobody happy." Check out the forms at the end of this chapter. Taking a few minutes to fill out such forms and keeping them in a conveniently located binder, folder, or stacking tray can eliminate many daily annoyances.

De-Junking Your House

Dejunking one's home seems like a daunting task the first time you do it, but every time after that it's merely maintenance. I put this job in my tickler file as a semi-annual job. The first time it may take a couple of long days or you might commit to 20 minute dejunking sessions daily for a few weeks.

The general rule of thumb is this: If you haven't used it, needed it, worn it, or enjoyed looking at it in the last year, then GET RID OF IT!

You will need:

- Several boxes of uniform size (paper boxes work nicely or plastic tubs) for things that will be in the "Just store it" category
- 2 large black trash bags and label one of them "Unload it" and one of them "New owners"

Now, pick a room! I take my box and my bags into each room of the house and ask myself the following questions:

Is it out of place? (Put it in the "Just store it" box)

Is it still usable? (Put it in the "Unload it" bag if it's not)

Is it usable, but no one in our home needs it? (Put it in the "New owners" bag and give it away)

Is it nostalgic? If there is a special memory attached to it and someone in the family will need therapy one day if I get rid of it, then- (Put it back and Keep it)

After every room in the house has been tackled in this manner, organize your storage boxes. Using the boxes described above, label them Box 1, Box 2, etc. Then in Section 5 of your tickler file you assign each box a 3x5 card with a corresponding number. For example:

Box 1: Snowman Decoration

Box 2: St. Patrick's Day Decorations

Box 3: Easter Decorations

.

.

.

Box 10: Ben's Winter 3T clothes

.

.

.

Box 14: Special Kitchen items: canning utensils, lefse rolling pin, etc.

Boxes 15a, 15b, 15c, 15d, etc. are reserved for income tax materials to coordinate with the filing deadline of April 15th. Boxes 25a, 25b, 25c, 25d, etc. are reserved for Christmas decorations. Be specific as you label these boxes. Be as detailed as possible so that you know exactly where to find your stockings, nativity set, or advent calendar if necessary.

Forms that Follow:

Family History

Shopping Guide

Items Loaned and Borrowed

Important Numbers

Call/Do/See

Internet Password Checklist

Credit Cards

Resources:

Arndt, Elise. *A Mother's Time*. Saratoga Publishing,1996.

Barnes, Emilie. *More Hours In My Day*. Harvest House, 1982.

Cilley, Marla. *Sink Reflections*. Bantam, 2002.

Eisenberg, Ronni. *Organize Your Home*. Hyperion, 1994.

Family Circle 2000 Hints and Tips, Doubleday, 2000

Martin, Gail. *What Every Child Should Know Along the Way*. GFI, 1999.

Otto, Donna, *Get More Done in Less Time*. Harvest House, 1994.

Penshorn, Cathy. *Juggling Tasks, Tots, and Time*. Zondervan, 2001.

Savage, Jill. *Professionalizing Motherhood*. Zondervan, 200

Family History

Family Member Name	Birth Date	Social Security Number	Clinic Number	Date of Last Physical	Date of Last Dental Exam	Date of Last Eye Exam	Vaccination/Date

Shopping Guide

Family Member	Dress/Suit Size	Shoe Size	Pants Size	Socks Size	Underwear Size	Shirt Size

Items Loaned and Borrowed

Month/Year	Item	Who	Returned

Credit Cards

Company	Card Number	Company Address	Company Phone Number	Expiration Date	Interest Rate	Amount Owed

Important Numbers

Service Person	Phone Number	Service Person	Phone Number
Ambulance		Neighbor	
Appliance Repair		Neighbor	
Dentist		Orthodontist	
Doctor		Pastor	
Doctor		Pastor	
Electrician		Poison Control	
Fire		Police	
Gas Co. - Emergency		Plumber	
Heating/AC Repair		School	
Husband's Work		School	
Insurance (car)		Veterinarian	
Insurance (home)		Babysitter	
		Babysitter	

Internet Passwords

Website Name	Website URL	Username	Date	Password

Date:_____

Call:

1_____

2_____

3_____

4_____

5_____

Do:

1_____

2_____

3_____

4_____

5_____

See:

1_____

2_____

3_____

4_____

5_____

Birthday Parties for Peanuts

"When she gave birth to a son she said,

'...I will praise the LORD'."

Genesis 29:35

Your child comes home from a friend's or a classmate's party talking non-stop about how much fun it was to jump in the inflatable castle and to ride on the ponies. Ponies? As a parent you get a sick feeling in the pit of your stomach thinking, "How am I going to afford a party for my child's birthday if I have to compete with ponies?" Today's birthday parties are more extreme and more expensive than when we were children. Each parent wants to provide "the best" birthday experience for their child which sometimes entails a lot of money and "exotic" locations.

In Rochester, birthday parties for children are being held at movie theaters, salons and spas, bowling alleys, horse riding stables, water parks, and even climbing walls! Games like Pin the Tail on the Donkey seem to have been forgotten, but perhaps it's time to bring them back.

If your budget and parenting style include keeping things simple and age appropriate, without taking out a small loan, then considering the following seven party principles will get you on the way to a great party experience. When everyone else is having "extreme" parties, a simple party will be different and kids love things to be different!

Party Principle #1: Friends...Less is More

When you are trying to determine who should be invited to a party and how many guests to include, realize that if you invite too many guests, the guest-of-honor will not be able to spend time with each guest. A common rule of measure is to invite the same number of guests as the age of the child. Some parents choose to add one or two children to this equation. So my 3-year-old birthday boy would be allowed to have three friends attend his party. However, as children get older this formula may require some revision. Take it from me, at my house eight little girls at a sleep over for an eight-year-old is TOO many! Only you know your limit however.

You might consider inviting special friends who your child doesn't see every day. Do not feel obligated, however, to invite siblings or even parents. Many parents will enjoy the break and you won't feel the additional pressure of entertaining and feeding adults.

While we are on the subject of who to invite, you also need to consider invitations. Mail your invitations two weeks before the party. It is best to specify the beginning and ending times for the party. Do not leave it open-ended. The best party times are 1:00 - 3:00 or 2:00 - 4:00 because you can avoid serving a meal. However, little ones don't last as long so shorten the party to one and a half hour and try 10:00am -11:30 to work around nap time.

Party Principle #2: Theme...Party Glue

A theme helps to focus the party, not to mention that it's just plain fun! It is quite easy to coordinate paper goods, a cake, goodie bags, and games around your theme.

Fun themes for girls include:

- Baking party: Girls each bake and decorate their own small cake, wearing bakers hats and personalized aprons (available at craft stores).

- Tea party: Girls enjoy dressing up and sipping tea from real china cups and eating fancy sandwiches and petite cakes. Miniature ready-to-paint tea sets are available at craft stores.

- Beading party: Girls 6 years and older love beads and jewelry. You can purchase beads at a hobby store or invite someone who has a bead business to do a party

for you. I have attended parties with this bead lady
and had marvelous results! I highly recommend her.
Bracelets etc. – Christine Kivi – 529-1994

- Lady Bug Party: Ages 3 – 6 Lady bug plates, lady bug
  cupcakes, making lady bug bean bags as a craft, and
  wearing ladybug antennae, all make this non-creepy
  party just plain cute!

Fun themes for boys include:

- Hot Wheels: The boys enjoy painting small wooden race
  cars from craft stores and racing them in the living
  room after it's been transformed into a racetrack out
  of cardboard, construction paper and pictures of race
  cars from an old car calendar. Serve Hot Wheel fruit
  snacks and play with a basket of cars on a mat.

- Construction party: Little boys love dirt so digging for
  treasures buried in the sandbox is tons of fun.
  Topped with yellow hard hats, boys will also enjoy
  tossing gray socks filled with beans into a toy dump
  truck across the room.

- Cowboy party: Saddle up for a stompin' good time! You might be thinking, "I thought she said we wouldn't have to rent a pony to really make our little horse lovers happy?!" I meant it! Set the mood with cowboy hats, red and white checkered table clothes, and country music. Give each child a balloon tied to a real horseshoe, and make faux leather vests out of brown paper bags.

- Train Party: All aboard to celebrate a birthday! Dress your birthday boy as an engineer and pass out a bandanna to each guest as they arrive. Make a sheet cake and use shoestring licorice for a track and add a toy train on top. A whistle makes a fun party favor! (Okay, their parents might not agree!)

Fun Themes for Anyone:

- Ytrap Sdrawkcab: It's a Backwards Party. The idea is to do everything backwards! Greet your incoming guests with "Thank you for coming to my birthday party. Please come again! Bye!" Open presents first. Sing "You to Birthday Happy." Give game prizes out to each child BEFORE playing the game and say "Everybody clap, Caleb did such a good job!" Then play the game, backwards of course!

- Glow in the Dark Party: Have this party at night and include flashlights, glow necklaces and bracelets, glow in the dark craft glue and face paint. You can even find glow-in-the-dark balls and Band-Aids!

- Balloon party: Make homemade invitations and attach a balloon and write, "Just Burstin' To Share My Birthday with You!" Decorations couldn't be easier with lots of helium balloons. There are countless balloon games and a balloon-shaped cake is pretty simple to create.

- Color party: This is cute and has endless possibilities. Choose a color and have all the plates, napkins, cups, clothing, streamers, balloons, food, and guests in that color.

Party Principle #3: Food for Fun

Three things to remember when choosing kid-friendly food are; make it fun to look at, easy to pick up, and tasty. What you serve will depend on the age of the guests you are inviting. For young children you will want to serve easy finger foods that won't be too hard on your floors when it is dropped. (Notice that I said "when" and not "if." That is experience talking!) For this age you need to serve things that won't be a choking hazard like hot dogs cut length-wise into quarters, vegetable or fruit pieces and dip, chips, luncheon meats, cheese chunks, Cheerios, mini muffins, slices of apple... whatever the kids like to eat. Your kids will enjoy some of these fun recipes!

Apple Smiles

- *1 or more apples*
- *Peanut butter*
- *Mini-marshmallows*

Cut apple into wedges, spread peanut butter on one side of each wedge. Place 4 mini-marshmallows on peanut butter of one wedge, and place another wedge on top. It looks like a smile with teeth!

Caramel Dip for Apples

- 1 8-ounce package of cream cheese (softened to room temperature)
- 1 cup brown sugar
- 1 teaspoon vanilla
- Apples

Mix together well. Chill about 15 minutes. Slice apples and dunk away!

Edible Jewelry

- 2 cups Fruit Loops
- 2/3 cup Cheerios
- 2 packages gummy lifesavers
- A piece of shoestring licorice for each child

Tie a knot in the end of each piece of licorice, and give one to each child. Lay the goodies out for children to alternately string on the licorice to form an edible necklace. When licorice is strung with jewels, tie the ends together so the necklace can be worn and eaten at the same time!

Special Spiders

- Ritz crackers
- Peanut butter
- Raisins
- Thin pretzel sticks

Spread peanut butter on one side of the cracker. Add two raisins (eyes) side by side near the edge of the cracker. Break four pretzel sticks in half. Place four pretzels on each side of the cracker to be spider legs.

Aquariums

- Graham crackers
- Blue icing
- Goldfish crackers

Spread the icing on the graham crackers and top with the goldfish.

Granola Bars

- 2-1/2 cup rice cereal (i.e. Rice Krispies)
- 2 cups oatmeal (I think old fashioned rolled oats work best)
- 1/2 cup raisins

- 1/2 cup corn syrup
- 1/2 cup brown sugar
- 1/2 cup peanut butter
- 1/2 cup chocolate chips
- 1 teaspoon vanilla
- 1 teaspoon cinnamon (optional)

In a mixing bowl, mix cereal, oatmeal, and raisins. In a saucepan, mix brown sugar and corn syrup. Stirring constantly, bring to a boil. Once boiling, remove from heat and add peanut butter, vanilla, and cinnamon, if desired. Then, mix with cereal mixture. Let mixture cool for 10 min, then add chocolate chips. Spread into 9x13" pan. When completely cool, cut into bars.

Dominoes

- Graham crackers
- Vanilla frosting
- Chocolate chips or M&Ms

Break graham crackers into fourths. Frost crackers and lightly cut a line through the frosting in the center of the cracker. Add chocolate chips or M&Ms on each side of the domino. This is a great way to count or do addition.

Cheeseburger Cookies

- *1 box vanilla wafers (buns)*
- *1 package Keebler grasshopper cookies (meat)*
- *Coconut died green (lettuce)*
- *Powdered sugar*
- *Milk*
- *Red and yellow food coloring*

Mix powdered sugar, milk, red and yellow food coloring to make orange cheese frosting. Mix more powdered sugar and milk to make "mayo". Put orange "cheese" on 1 vanilla wafer and press together with a grasshopper cookie. Cover second vanilla wafer with "mayo" and sprinkle with green coconut. Put a thin layer of frosting on the grasshopper cookie and press all three together.

Party Principle #4: Entertainment: Simple & Sensational

Children remember what they did at a party much more than what they ate. Plan to do things that kids don't do every day. When considering games remember that no one should go home a loser! Competitive games are enjoyable only for the people who win. A party should be fun. Avoid tears by selecting games at which everyone gets a chance to be successful. Better yet, plan a few cooperative games, in which the whole group faces a challenge. Most kids love a great treasure map that will lead them to a treasure that they can split evenly.

Party Games

Here are some fun on-the-spot games that require only a few, inexpensive materials.

- Catch a balloon
- Chalk drawing on the sidewalk
- Bubble gum blowing contest
- Before kids come, hide peanuts or some other small objects in the yard and have a hunt.
- Teams race to melt ice cubes the fastest without putting them in their mouths.

- Guess the number of jellybeans in a jar

- Play "I packed my bags and took a _____." (This is similar to the alphabet game, but items do not necessarily have to be in alphabetical order.)

- Beanbag relay — balance beanbags on their heads, necks, elbows, etc.

- M&M relay — scoop the candy from one bowl, race to the other side of the room and deposit what is left on the spoon in another dish.

- Freeze dance

- Hot Potato

- Duck, Duck, Gray Duck (otherwise known as Duck, Duck, Goose — depending on where you grew up!)

- Sing

- Play categories: say "Fruit" and kids name fruits until they run out

- Tag

- Red, Red, Red: Kids stand behind a line and when the leader says "red, red, blue" they can not run. When the leader says "red, red, red" they run toward the leader.

- Red Light, Green Light: Similar to Red, Red, Red. Kids stand behind a line and when the leader says "Red light" he faces the kids and they can not run. When he says "Green light" he turns his back to the kids and they run like crazy. The leader turns quickly to say "Red light" and catch the kids running. Runners who get caught go back to the line

- "What Time is it, Mr. Fox?" - Kids ask, "What time is it, Mr. Fox?" The leader says a time between 1 and 11 o'clock. The children move that number of steps and try to get as close to the fox without touching him. When the fox shouts, "Midnight!" the children must try to run back to the line without getting tagged.

- Find the Color: The leader says, "I see the color _____. Can you find it?" Then the leader counts down from a given number to zero. The children hop, skip, or run to touch something that color.

- Mirrors: Two kids face each other and one child initiates motion and the other attempts to match his or her partner.

- Set up activity stations. The stations do not have to be elaborate or expensive. The birthday child can pick what they want to do. For example, you might have

Legos at one station, a dollhouse at another, play dough at a station and a craft activity at another. You should not need more than four stations. Prepare all of the activities and games before the party. This allows you to focus on the kids when the party begins.

- A Pull-String Pinata: Watching children behead a favorite character, in order to enjoy candy and treasures, is not my idea of fun. Invariably someone gets whacked with a stick and ends up in tears. However, with a pull string piñata and extra bags of goodies, a piñata can be a pleasant party activity even for young children. Instead of hitting the piñata, there are strings attached to a hidden door. When pulled, one of these strings will open the piñata, releasing the candy. Most store-bought piñatas can be converted to pull-string style using the following instructions:

1. Place the piñata with the bottom facing up.

2. On the bottom, use a utility knife to make a 3-sided trap door with approximately 3 to 4 inch sides.

3. Use the point of the blade to make small slits through the cardboard on the flap. Make a slit for each ribbon that you plan to use (at least one for each guest).

4. Thread a ribbon through each slit. Ribbon length should vary according to the height at which you plan to hang your piñata.

5. If you want all of the children to open the piñata at the same time, knot all of the ribbons (inside the flap). Traditionally, one or two ribbons are knotted, leaving the rest loose.

6. Fill the piñata with candy and/or small prizes.

7. Close the flap and lightly seal with a small piece of Scotch tape, using enough to hold the flap shut but not so much as to prevent the door from opening when the ribbon(s) is pulled.

8. The children take turns pulling one ribbon at a time. One ribbon will open the piñata flap.

Party Principle #5: Cake is the Highlight

This is the party moment that everyone loves the best. You can seal the success of your child's party by allowing him/her to choose the flavor and type of cake that they want for themselves. Plan to make this cake yourself. Most hobby stores carry different shaped cake pans from Scooby Doo to Bob the Builder. The library has lots of cake decorating books. Making this a themed creation is half the fun. Not a baker you say? You might consider an alternative to cake like cupcakes with different toppings that the children may choose from, or even baking cupcakes in an ice cream cone! How about brownies, a giant cookie, a favorite pie, or doughnuts? Remember that kids like to be different!

Ice Cream Cone Cakes

- *1 package of cake mix (i.e. Betty Crocker SuperMoist Party Rainbow Chip)*
- *24 flat-bottom ice cream cones*
- *1 tub ready to spread frosting*
- *Toppings such as Cheerios, animal crackers, miniature chocolate chips, dried fruit, candy sprinkles, crushed hard candies, graham cracker crumbs, or chopped nuts.*

Heat oven to 350 degrees. Place paper baking cup in each of 24 regular size muffin cups. Prepare cake mix as directed on the package, except fill each cup 2/3 full of batter (1 heaping tablespoon each). Place ice cream cone upside-down on batter in each cup. Bake 20 minutes (cones may tilt on the batter); cool completely. Remove paper baking cups. Frost cakes with frosting and decorate with Toppings as desired.

Party Principle #6: Theme-related Favors are Fun

When choosing party favors, it's better to spend more creativity than money. Each guest can be given several little goodies or one larger item that has to do with the party—a flowerpot and seeds for a garden party or candy tied up in a bandanna for a cowboy party. Pencils, stickers, gum, and candy are all popular prizes. Rub-on-tattoos, stick-on-earrings, and plastic jewelry are also hits. You can even send the guests home with an item they have made during the party. The birthday child should hand out the favors. This will remind him or her to say "thank you" to their guests.

Party Principle # 7: Receiving Gifts

Before every birthday party we remind our children that receiving gifts is more about the giver than the gift. When children give gifts to their friends, it is terribly important to them that it is received well. It is our responsibility to remind the birthday child that the gift givers have spent much thought, time, and sometimes money on these gifts. For the birthday child to be kind to their friends they should be appreciative of and enthusiastic about every gift. For young children, especially under 5, it is sometimes better to open the gifts after the party to avoid potential conflicts. Young children sometimes believe that because they brought the gift it belongs to them. Tug-of-war over a gift is one activity most parents prefer to avoid.

Party Pictures

Take lots of pictures and then send extras with thank you notes to your guests. Use a telephoto lens and focus on those natural shots when you catch kids in activities. Also, try different angles; kneel down to the kids' level, horizontal and vertical shots. Your kids will cherish these pictures when they are older.

Party Safety

Define your party-area boundaries. If you are inside, tell the kids which rooms they may occupy. If you are outside, establish the limits of the yard. If necessary, mark the perimeter with something bright, like ribbon, a hose, cones, or flags. Put away potential hazards or troublemakers like charcoal lighter fluid, garden chemicals, and toys that may be fought over or used as weapons. Plan activities, being proactive can eliminate many potential problems. Just in case though, be sure you have a first aid kit available, and if parents are not staying with the children, be sure you have phone numbers where they can be reached at all times. Finally, ask a friend, family member or neighbor to help with the party. The smaller the ratio of children to adults, the more likely you will be able to prevent accidents from happening.

More Ideas for Making Birthdays Special

- The night before your child's birthday, after they are asleep, release balloons in their bedroom and tie streamers to the bedpost.

- Make a flag for each child in your home that can be hung outside your front door. The flag should announce, "Today is ___'s Birthday!" Decorate the flag with symbols and pictures that reflect his/her personality. Then save the flag to be hung outside every year!

- Arrange a treasure hunt for the presents that will be given by the family.

- Allow the birthday child to "order" breakfast or make it a family breakfast out at a favorite restaurant. This can be done for lunch or dinner too.

- Relieve your birthday child of chores for the day.

- Call grandparents or other special people who live far away.

- Make a birthday tablecloth. I suggest using a linen tablecloth and pens that will be permanent on fabric (available at hobby stores). Have the birthday child sign their name and trace their handprints or draw a picture that best represents who they are right now. Only take out this tablecloth on birthdays.

- Make a big production of completing a birthday form annually to commemorate and celebrate changes in your child. This form records sizes, favorites, likes and dislikes, friends, hobbies, handwriting or drawing abilities, and much more. If you save these forms in a scrapbook or baby book you and your child will enjoy looking at these for many years. I have included a sample for you at the end of this chapter.

Most importantly, remember to have fun and enjoy the celebration of your child's birth!

These party ideas were based on parties we have had in our home, attended, or I have clipped from magazines and filed for future celebrations. There are many party books available at the library, but I have found the Internet to be the best source for additional ideas and resources. Keywords: Children's Birthday Parties, Birthday Party

Birthday Survey

1. What is your favorite toy to play with?

2. What is your favorite color?

3. What is your favorite book?

4. What is your favorite food?

5. What is your favorite song?

6. What is your favorite family time activity?

7. What is your favorite thing to imagine?

8. How do you like to sleep (comfort item or place)?

9. What are your favorite clothes to wear?

10. What time did you wake up and who was the first to wish you a happy birthday?

11. How did you spend your birthday this year?

12. What was your favorite gift you received?

13. What was your cake like?

14. What would you like to do on your next birthday?

How you write your name _____

How old are you today? _____

Today's Date is _____

Family Resource

Numbers

ABUSE

National Child Abuse Hot Line   800-422-4453

Women's Shelter Inc.   285-1010 or 800-438-6439

COMMUNITY/SOCIAL/HUMAN SERVICES

Catholic Charities-Rochester Office   280-2180

Channel One Food Bank & Food Shelf   287-2350

Christmas Anonymous   285-3940

Community Housing Partnership   281-7396 or

800-621-8303

Legal Assistance of Olmsted County   287-2036

March of Dimes   888-663-4637

New Life Family Services   282-3377

Ronald McDonald House   282-3955

CRISIS INTERVENTION/COUNSELING SERVICES

Victim Services   285-8242

Poison Control Center   800-764-7661

HEALTH/MENTAL HEALTH/DISABILITIES

Ability Building Center   281-6262

Hiawatha Homes   289-7222

REM River Bluffs   289-3319

Rehab Services   285-7293

Zumbro Valley Mental Health Center   281-6240 or

                                                 800-422-0161

OLMSTED COUNTY

Financial Services   285-8382

    Energy Assistance

    Food Stamps

    General Assistance

    Medical Assistance

    Minnesota Supplemental/Aid

    Refugees

Social Services   285-7009

Olmsted County Human Rights   287-1347

PUBLIC HEALTH

Public Health Services   285-8370

Water and Radon Analysis   285-8370

Health Education Services   285-8370

Public Health Clinics   285-8370
    Immunization
    Family Planning
    Pregnancy Testing
    Child Health Clinic

WIC (Women Infants & Children Nutrition Program)   285-8336

PARENTING RESOURCES

New Life Family Services   282-3377

902 N. Broadway

Christian, nonprofit center providing pregnancy and adoption

counseling. Abstinence education, free pregnancy testing,

maternity clothing closet, support groups

Child Care Resource & Referral   287-2020

26 Woodlake Drive SE

Primary goal is to ensure that all children have access to

quality, nurturing environment for child care

Community-based organization that delivers person-to-person services that include child care referrals and training for parents and child care givers

La Leche League

An international, nonprofit, nonsectarian organization dedicated in providing education, information, support and encouragement to women who want to breastfeed

Good Shepherd Lutheran Church   289-1748

559 20th Street SW

Meets third Tuesday at 7:00 p.m.

Grace Evangelical Free Church   533-4704

1st Street E, Stewartville,

Meets first Thursday at 10:00 a.m.

PAIIR   285-8033

201 8th Street NW

Parents Are Important In Rochester-Strengthening families with young children through education and support

- Offer a variety of parent/child classes from birth through school-age
- Class fees vary
- Call to receive a catalog of classes

Pipsqueaks   287-2000

United Way Building

903 W. Center Street NW

- Indoor playground as a part of the City Park & Recreation system
- Ages infants through Kindergarten-must be accompanied by adult
- Open during the school year

Hours: Monday-Friday 9 a.m.-12 noon

Tuesday-Thursday 1 p.m.-5 p.m

Saturday 9 a.m.-4 p.m.

MOPS (Mothers of Preschoolers)   www.mops.org

- Nonprofit organization for any mom who shares a similar desire to be the best mom she can be
- Moms "graduate" from the program when their youngest child completes Kindergarten
- A time to come and fellowship with other moms in this season of life
- Guest speakers, crafts, discussion groups, and food during a 22 hour time period

- Moppets-a children's program runs concurrently during moms meeting time
- A membership fee for the year

Berean Community Church   289-4179

3157 Kenosha Drive NW

Daytime-meet second and fourth Tuesdays beginning September through May from 9 a.m. - 11:00 a.m.

Moppets-a children's program runs concurrently during moms meeting time

A membership fee for the year

Calvary Baptist Church   289-6750

5905 Silas Dent Rd. NW

Daytime-meet second Wednesday beginning September through May

Evening-meet fourth Tuesday beginning September through May

Christ Community Church   282-5569

4400 55th Street NW

Daytime-meet first and third Tuesdays beginning September through May from 9 a.m.- 11:15 a.m.

Childcare provided at minimal cost

Evening-meet first and third Tuesdays beginning

September through May from 6:30 p.m.- 8:30 p.m.;

limited childcare provided at minimal cost

First Baptist Church   288-8880

415 16th Street SW

Daytime -meet first and third Thursdays beginning

September through May from 9:15 a.m.- 11:30 a.m.

Childcare provided at minimal cost

Mothers & More   www.mothersandmore.org

- A nonprofit organization dedicated to improving the lives of mothers through support, education, and advocacy
- Addresses mothers needs as individuals and members of society and promote the value of all the work mothers do
- Guest speakers, play groups, Mom's Night Out

Coldwell Banker/Burnett Building   259-8948

140 Elton Hills Drive NW

Meet the second and fourth Tuesdays at 7:15 p.m.

A Mother's Heart & Moms in Touch

Berean Community Church   289- 4179

3157 Kenosha Drive NW

- Moms in Touch provides an opportunity to come and pray with other home-school moms for your school and family

- 6:30 p.m.

- A Mother's Heart is a home-school support group meeting the last Monday of the month

- 7:15 p.m.- 9:00 p.m.; refreshments provided

Southern MN Mothers of Multiples

www.geocities.com/mothersofmultiples

Support group for mothers raising twins, triplets or more

Stop Telemarketing

Telephone Preference Service Address

Direct Marketing Association

P.O. Box 9008

Farmingdale, NY 11735-9008

Minnesota "Do Not Call" list

www.commerce.state.mn.us

1-800-921-4110

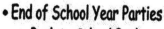